Frith's Encounters

Personal Insights and Friendships from Rhodes to Roebuck

By David Frith

vKp
Von Krumm Publishing

First published in Great Britain by
VON KRUMM PUBLISHING
21 Sackville Rd
Hove BN3 3WA
www.vonkrummpublishing.co.uk

796.358

A CIP record of this book is available from the British Library.

Cover and all interior graphic design by Stewart Karl Davies

Printed and Bound in Great Britain by
Berforts Information Press Ltd. Stevenage

ISBN 978-0-9567321-2-5

Other Books By David Frith

Runs in the Family (with John Edrich)
"My Dear Victorious Stod": a Biography of A.E.Stoddart
The Archie Jackson Story
The Fast Men
Cricket Gallery (ed.)
Great Moments in Cricket (as "Andrew Thomas", with Norman Harris)
England v Australia: a Pictorial History of the Test Matches since 1877
The Ashes '77 (with Greg Chappell)
The Golden Age of Cricket
The Illustrated History of Test Cricket (with Martin Tyler)
The Ashes '79
Thommo (with Jeff Thomson)
Rothmans Presents 100 Years England v Australia (co-edited)
The Slow Men
Cricket's Golden Summer: Paintings in a Garden (with Gerry Wright)
England v Australia Test Match Records 1877-1985 (ed.)
Pageant of Cricket
Guildford Jubilee 1938-1988
By His Own Hand
Stoddy's Mission: the First Great Test Series 1894-95
Test Match Year 1996-97 (ed.)
Caught England, Bowled Australia (autobiography)
The Trailblazers: the First English Cricket Tour of Australia 1861-62
Silence of the Heart: Cricket's Suicides
Bodyline Autopsy
The Ross Gregory Story
Battle for the Ashes [2005]
The Battle Renewed: the Ashes Regained 2006-07
The David Frith Archive
Inside Story [Australian Cricket Board history] (with Gideon Haigh)
Frith on Cricket (anthology)
Cricket's Collectors
Guildford's Cricket Story

For the best and most important
"encounter" of them all:
Oriel, known as Debbie

First, The Briefer
Encounters, Handshakes
And Conversations

THERE SEEMS to be something slightly mystic about shaking hands with distinguished people, whether the clasp be casual or firm. Beyond those vague theories about DNA being transferable, the intriguing old musing about being One Handshake Away From . . . is worth a thought. A handshake with **Don Bradman** was a flesh-touch away from several monarchs, or from Charlie Bannerman, who back in 1877 scored a century in the first of all Test matches, or even Babe Ruth, or Winston Churchill. The Don touched flesh with them all, and countless thousands of others besides.

"Shake the hand that shook the hand of..." is all well and good, but getting to know interesting or celebrated people (in that strict order of priority) is even more rewarding. In just over sixty years of devotion to cricket I've gone out of my way to meet players from across the ages, because while statistics are the framework or skeleton of the game, *people* are cricket's *flesh and blood*. The character/personality is what matters. That's not to say that I've gained no satisfaction besides in finding hundreds of cricketers' graves, starting with Victor Trumper's. While not exactly encounters, there was often something vaguely spiritual about the experience.

From a distance, I caught sight of **Winston Churchill** and **Field Marshal Montgomery** during the 1945 Victory parade in London, while the first "celebrity" (ghastly species/classification) I ever spoke to, a couple of years later, was **Prince Monolulu**, the colourful racing tipster ("I've got a horse!"), who was dining at the Soho restaurant where my father was manager. That cosy Rupert Street establishment was frequented by film stars and boxers and shysters, but no cricketers.

With cricket absorbing me for most of my life, all these years down the line I treasure and draw great warmth from the contact I've had with hundreds of renowned players, one of whom, **Wilfred Rhodes**, took me by means of his rasping Yorkshire narrative back into the late 19th Century. Shake the hand that shook the hand of a man who dismissed W.G.Grace – more than once too. What stories, previously unrecorded in print, have been unfurled. Insights into the real person have been unveiled. What delight I've had from these encounters, many of which deepened into on-going friendship.

The idea of putting together some essays recalling the most interesting cricketers I've known was sparked by John Stern, who was then editor of the magazine *The Wisden Cricketer*. This publication was a sort of bastard child of the old magazine *The Cricketer* (founded 1921) and *Wisden Cricket Monthly*. I had edited both, the first from 1972 to 1978, the second from 1979, when I founded it, until 1996, when I left – not entirely of my own volition, following some dark manoeuvres by persons whose identities I shall protect, though they hardly deserve it. A freelance again, some years later I was seated next to John throughout the Perth Test of the 2006-07 whitewash Ashes series (I was writing a book on that tour), and my occasional, perhaps frequent, reflections on cricketers from ages past caused him, on the final day of the Test, to speculate that there might be potential in these ramblings as a series in the magazine.

I needed no encouragement. My Don Bradman memoir launched the series in the English spring of 2007. It was to run for almost five years, encouraged by John and his successor Ed Craig, before another of those inexplicable behind-the-scenes decisions halted it. There were still some Encounters waiting to be written. They are included in this book.

The qualification is that my acquaintance or friendship with the subjects had to be significant. And, somewhat poignantly, the subject had to have left this life behind. There is a very long and teasing sub-list of cricketers whom I have known or with whom I've had passing contact but who lend themselves to nothing more than the briefest of anecdotes rather than full-length Encounters. In most of these cases, while it was a delight to be in their presence, nothing all that meaningful transpired.

The most extreme instance of this was when I spent half-an-hour or so sitting alongside the record-holding South African batsman **Bruce Mitchell** at a barbecue during his country's Test Centenary celebrations in 1989. That privileged opportunity elicited nothing more than an occasional whispered half-sentence. This was in contrast to **Eric Rowan**, a batsman of equal rank but opposite temperament: he seemed to be glaring at everybody in the vicinity as if desirous of a punch-up, and rasped one provocative remark after another. His brother **Athol**, a war veteran, was very different: genial and relaxed. There were many other South African veterans, such as **"Tuppy" Owen-Smith**, and **Ossie Dawson**, with whom it was a delight to have brief sessions For another memorable half-hour I sat talking to **Neil Adcock** and **Peter Heine**, the Springbok terror bowlers, who were both charming and far removed from the monster figures of the 1950s. One extraordinary remark was recorded in *Wisden Cricket Monthly*. But there was not enough substance in any of these for a full essay. There was also a tender meeting with **Jackie McGlew**, whom I'd watched occupying the crease doggedly at Sydney back in 1952-53. He was very polite, but clearly struggling with his health. Like many of the veterans, he was glad of the support for what they were trying to accomplish to resolve their country's huge difficulties.

One morning during those Centenary celebrations, as the bus rumbled to the cricket ground, I had my birthday toasted by seven former South Africa and England Test captains: with vintage port in plastic cups. There were handshakes all round in a week of handshakes all round as long-forgotten South African Test cricketers and others from around the globe continued to appear. A man might have finished up with bruised hands.

This right mitt of mine has also shaken the hands of **Bill Ponsford** (the only batsman to have reached 400 twice until Brian Lara came along: "It'll cost ya," the laconic Ponny murmured when asked to sign a book), as well as Bradman's first Test captain **Jack Ryder** (he died a few days later, following the Centenary Test match in Melbourne), and the Bodyline umpires **George Borwick** and **George Hele**, and **Clarrie Grimmett** (who later confessed to me in a letter that he was one year older than the records showed). **Laurie Nash**, 1930s tearaway fast bowler and Aussie Rules super-hero, is someone I remember for his pugnacious attitude and, alas, bad breath. Then came another rare handshake with **"Nip" Pellew**, a member of the mighty 1921 Australian side, soldier in the First World War, a fieldsman who sometimes lost the heel off a boot as he raced around the outfield, so swiftly did he travel and so committedly did he stretch for the ball.

Dozens of others were all around us day after day during those fabulous 1977 Centenary Test celebrations in Melbourne. But there was not enough for an Encounter when the contact was simply a smile, a handshake, a signature in a book, a brief exchange. As a bonus during that unforgettable Melbourne Centenary event I found myself chatting with surprise guests **Bert Sutcliffe**,

John Reid, **Walter Hadlee** and **Merv Wallace**, top-shelf New Zealand cricketers who had crossed the Tasman as special guests at the festivities. Some years later I was lucky enough to attend a reunion dinner for Australian Services cricketers, who were joined by **Martin Donnelly**, a charming, urbane New Zealand and Oxford University left-hander whose batting had touched sublime heights just after the Second World War.

These airmen and soldiers were a breed apart, and I wistfully think of them when watching, head in hands, the petulant, infantile behaviour of many of the modern cricketers.

The links between cricket and showbiz have long been strong, perhaps because of the similarity in the strain of public performance. It has been amusing to see Test cricketers and television big names together, for they nearly always shrink into a state of mutual respect bordering on awe – or at least an understanding of the demands each faces almost daily/nightly. At Lord's Taverners events, like the golf day, **Harry Secombe** was a scream. He liked a big peak to his cricket cap because he could use it for slicing the cake at teatime. I once sat for some time with **Spike Milligan** in a Lord's box, listening to his proud recall of playing Army rugby on the sacred turf of Twickenham. As with many clowns, there was a detectable underlying sadness. We sat at **Eric Morecambe's** table once at a Taverners dinner, and this funniest of Englishmen became quite serious as his heart problem became the subject of conversation. My wife, Debbie, had experience in health and dietary matters and was able to put suggestions to him which he seemed to find interesting. Still, though, he was compulsively making jokes every couple of minutes. In retrospect, the evening took on a deep poignancy.

Someone who was a devout cricket-lover besides being a world figure in cinema and stage was **Peter O'Toole**, who used to net regularly at Lord's. After his performance in *Pygmalion* in Guildford, I went to see him backstage. He was exhausted, but managed to exchange a few pleasantries and sign the programme for a fellow Taverner. Some time afterwards he was in the audience at the National Film Theatre when I presented the annual cricket film show. I was rather glad I didn't know he was there until afterwards. At the post-show drinkies he was nice enough to come over and say simply: "The important thing is to know when to talk and when to stop. Well done." I hope my thanks were expressed adequately. "Lawrence of Arabia" O'Toole was accompanied that night by **Harold Pinter**, and the playwright was last seen swishing his walking stick and growling obscenities at the people who were inadvertently blocking his exit through the crowded NFT foyer.

I think back to a British Film Institute luncheon when I was thrilled to be seated alongside **Trevor Howard**, but he uttered/mumbled no more than half-a-dozen words, a considerable let-down, in fact a "brief encounter". In retrospect, what could I have expected of a man who apparently fabricated his war record? A more rewarding BFI function was the banquet in honour of Orson Welles. I didn't get near the great and gargantuan man that night, but do recall having a cricket chat with **Peggy Ashcroft,** a stage and screen eminence who might perhaps have fitted John Arlott's twinkle-eyed summary of some other lively lady: "She wasn't all that keen on cricket but was very fond of cricketers".

Further showbiz "touches" came with a chat to **Tommy Trinder** at the stage door of the Tivoli Theatre in Sydney in the early 1950s. My mate Gus, from Essex, was with me, and I think the talk was mostly about football, a game which was once a big part of my life but which I now despise. Tommy, Fulham FC devotee, had played a fireman in the wartime film *The Bells Go Down*, doing on-screen what my heroic Dad had done in real life during the Blitz. Then there was **Guy Mitchell**, after his performance in Guildford a few years ago. His music had buoyed me through my youth, and I told him I'd gone to his concert at the old Sydney Stadium back in 1954 and bought a pair of Mitchell Blue socks. "Gee, I loved Sydney," he said. "Hey, can you get me back there for a concert maybe?" He'd greatly over-estimated my powers of influence. A year or two later we went backstage after **Slim Whitman** had sung in Woking. This time the talk was of Queensland and country music, especially *The Song of the Old Water Wheel* and *China Doll*. It doesn't hurt a man to get away from all-embracing cricket once in a while.

It does indeed take all sorts. What a lovable and ebullient man was **Patrick Moore**, the heavyweight astronomer and leg-spin bowler. He came to play in a charity match I organised in the late 1970s, but his floating spinners failed to touch the pitch because it was pouring rain and the ball was like a slippery bar of soap. Up it went into the stratosphere, seemingly on its way to join his beloved planets. This gigantic fellow in his tent-like sweater battled bravely on until, anxious about his well-being, I urged him to go off and dry himself out before pneumonia took hold. Pointing to a banner on the boundary which proclaimed "Patrick Moore for England", he stated indignantly that "these people have paid to see us and I shall perform my duty!" Meanwhile, my wife gazed at Patrick's watch, which he had entrusted to her while out in the sodden field, saying that Neil Armstrong had given it to him and it had been on the Moon. Debbie couldn't bring herself to wash that wrist for some days afterwards.

Way back in the 1950s there had been the briefest of contact with the reclusive little batting genius **Charlie Macartney** in Bert Oldfield's shop in Sydney, sustained long enough for him to inscribe my little autograph book. A couple of visits to **Stan McCabe's** sports shop around the corner in George Street elicited little more from that shy batting maestro than half-smiles as the merchandise was perused.

A chat with **Learie Constantine** in the old Lord's press-box above the Warner Stand mainly on the subject appropriate for both of us – attachment to two countries – was especially rewarding. Then, years later, there was the special gathering of West Indies veterans in Barbados in 1981, when pre-war players such as **Teddy Hoad** and a once-so-very-young Test cap **Derek Sealy** were present. Conversations were brief and necessarily superficial, although I did manage to spend precious time with **George Headley**, the gist of which comes later.

Also gratifying, when I was a guest of Surrey's then president **Alf Gover**, was a handshake in the committee-room at The Oval in 1980 with **Greville Stevens**, scorer of 466 not out in a college house match in 1919 and also one of the illustrious England XI which won the Ashes in 1926. A conversation with him stopped short of daring to ask him to confirm that he had taken off with Arthur Gilligan's wife some years before. As a naval officer in the war he could be excused almost anything.

When Guildford celebrated 50 years of county cricket in 1988 we invited all the survivors from that inaugural match in 1938 to the festivities surrounding the occasion, and the best part was sitting with them one evening at the local hotel. **Tom Barling** was in misty-eyed reflective mood, and little **Ted Whitfield**, who had scored a century in that first match, revelled in the memory and was good to listen to as he described cricket in a forgotten age. Meanwhile, **Monty Garland-Wells** sat glowering, and it occurred to me later that he was longing to enter the conversation but was waiting to be invited: which made little sense. I regretted not having asked him to talk us through his dismissal of Bradman in a Surrey v Australians match so long ago.

Much earlier, I had bought my first bat in England from the old Surrey player **Eddie Watts**, who was a stalwart figure, modest, affable, sometimes gently teasing. He had once taken all ten against Warwickshire in 1939, and now had a sports shop in Cheam. I spotted his beautifully-bound run of *Scores and Biographies* on a shelf, and embarked on a campaign to buy them from him. It was perhaps at the fourth approach that Eddie relented, and a deal was struck. After all, he never read them.

In the early 1950s, at the Sydney Cricket Ground, **K.S.Duleepsinhji**, then India's High Commissioner to Australia, elegant in double-breasted suit, strolled along the pathway at the back of the pavilion: but I was too shy to approach him even for an autograph. Many years later I acquired a letter which the young Indian had written to the mighty hitter G.L.Jessop early in 1930. In it he stated modestly that he did not expect to be chosen to play for England that summer. Shortly afterwards he was selected, and he stroked 173 against Australia at Lord's on Test debut.

Around that time, in the early 1950s, I joined a queue of youngsters lined up alongside a gleaming black Humber Super-Snipe in the SCG car park to get the autograph of cricket-loving Prime Minister of Australia **Robert Menzies**. Each in turn, we were urged to vote Liberal/Country Party when we were old enough. Many years later I had the dubious pleasure, at a Lord's Taverners lunch, of sitting next to another prime minister, **Edward Heath** (he who had got us tangled up with Europe, while turning away from our Commonwealth kith and kin). "Ted" seemed out of sorts this day and spoke little throughout the event. This was the cricket "fan" who followed Kent (I'd got his autograph in the Kent dressing-room the day they won the County Championship at The Oval in 1970) and who was mockingly "quoted" by at least one person as saying how much he adored the cricket of "Derek Knott" and "Alan Underwood".

Brian Statham is one I'd like to have known better, but apart from watching him playing in England's matches at Sydney, and bowling steep bouncers off three paces in the nets, and relaxing at the team hotel in Coogee, where he propped his sizable feet up on a table and asked the waiter for "Four more beers, please" (not all for himself), the clearest memory is of that easy-going Lancastrian, many years later and in unfamiliar dinner jacket, strolling down Park Lane and into the London Hilton for his testimonial dinner. We exchanged smiles, and he said: "I've just been stopped by a policeman. He seemed to think I were a terrorist."

A brief acquaintance with that magical spin bowler **Doug Wright** came rather too late. A gentle soul, during a gathering in 1995, in response to small-talk, he smiled vaguely and muttered a few observations, then wandered off. I was told that he frequently went jogging, but often returned up a driveway which wasn't his own. Fortunately, this bowler, who took a record seven first-class hat-tricks, has one of his gems preserved on film: bowling Lindsay Hassett with a medium-pace dipping leg-break. Another Kent player, **Tony Pawson**, became a staunch friend, but there is no Encounter here of Tony because he was simply a man of such extraordinary breadth of accomplishment in cricket, football, fly-fishing, journalism and business, and with a very interesting war record too, that he seems almost impossible to accommodate in the space available. Another Kent player, **Arthur Fagg**, the only batsman to score two double-centuries in the same match, was seen often on the circuit as a first-class and Test umpire, but any attempt to engage him in conversation fell flat.

When in Bundaberg during England's 1978-79 tour of Australia I located the general store run by **Don Tallon**, the wicketkeeper who was rated by Don Bradman as the very best. There was a slight problem in that "Deafy" Tallon was extremely hard of hearing. I tried a few openings, but, as with Arthur Fagg, it was plainly an interview that was not meant to be. I bought an ice cream and walked back over the river bridge. It was in contrast to a valued chance meeting at the SCG with **Colin McCool**, wartime commando and brilliant leg-spinning all-rounder who left Australia to make a name for himself all over again with Somerset. I've never known a Test cricketer to be so apparently interested in the person he was talking to: question after question. Of all the many cricketers mentioned in this book, McCool would be one of the Special Six to sit at my table. Only this time I'd insist on asking the questions.

During the 1987 World Cup, in Lahore, dear old **Shujauddin**, the Pakistan left-arm spinner, took a group of cricket writers to see the great fast-medium bowler **Fazal Mahmood**. That superb wicketkeeper-batsman **Imtiaz Ahmed** was there too, and I sat literally at the feet of Fazal as he described, one victim after another, how he mowed England down – Hutton, May, Compton, Graveney and the rest – in Pakistan's historic victory at The Oval back in 1954.

In 1974 there had been a bemusing incident one evening in Lahore when I was being driven back to the hotel in a Pakistan Cricket Board car. In the back sat the two umpires, both of whom were on Test debut. There had been five lbw dismissals in West Indies' first innings, and one of the umpires leaned forward to ask me if I knew what was the world Test record for lbws. I couldn't enlighten him, but his name hit the headlines some years later when he had a bust-up on the field with England skipper Mike Gatting. It was indeed **Shakoor Rana**.

The idolisation of top cricketers goes way back. As a schoolboy in Sydney, watching West Indies play, I had the thrill of speaking to **Frank Worrell** several times. The words are lost in time, and must have weighed very little. My pocket diary doesn't elaborate. But, down by the long-leg pickets, he was gracious in his response to the questions and observations. Later, leaning out from a window of the team bus, he signed a magazine photo for me with a flamboyant "Frankie Worrell". I've never seen a more elegant figure on a cricket field: maroon cap, cream/white shirt and flannels, gleaming black skin, clean bat, leisurely movement: and of course he was not splattered with garish commercial logos. How I wish I'd been privileged to have a sustained conversation, but what did I know at fourteen?

It might have been that same evening that a group of us sought more autographs, and one little chap blurted out: "Will you sign my book Clyde?" **Walcott**, in that basement-deep voice of his, rounded on the boy, having taken exception to the use of his first name: "Don't be so bloody presumptuous!" The lad ran off. I was still trying to reconcile this fifty years later when *Sir* Clyde Walcott, by then president of the International Cricket Council and preparing for a speech at some dinner, telephoned me to seek advice about obtaining some cricket joke books.

A year before that 1951-52 Australia v West Indies series I had had my baptism as a spectator at a Test match, when England played at Sydney. The first action I ever witnessed on a Test field was young substitute fieldsman **David Sheppard** scooping up the ball in the outfield and throwing in left-handed. Many years later I was pleased to be part of conversation groups at cricket functions, having earlier had a private and personal meeting with him at his Mayflower Centre in London's East End in the mid-1960s after my caring wife, sensing that all was not right in my world at that time, had got in touch with him. David's phone call was among the most unexpected incidents in a life replete with surprises. Of the "consultation" I remember next to nothing, cricket talk predominantly, but the trip was worthwhile. The future Bishop of

Liverpool must have given me something meaningful to work on.

That baptismal summer of 1950-51 embodied an incident of some significance, one which I've recited at every opportunity as I behold many a modern cricketer's dismissive attitude towards autograph-collectors. The hours spent patiently lingering by the great marble entrance columns of the Hotel Australia had ultimately been rewarded with all the English cricketers' signatures, with **Cyril Washbrook's** the most memorable. When I proffered one of the newly-invented biros, the stern Lancastrian ignored it. Instead, he reached into the inside pocket of his double-breasted suit, brought out his fountain-pen, and then dignified my autograph book with a bold and legible signature. Shame on the moderns who either brush fans aside or give them an absurd squiggle instead of a decent, legible "autograph".

A further echo from that 1950-51 Sydney Test – a seminal event which started me on a long and enthralling rollercoaster ride in the world of cricket – was the slap of the ball into Bedser's large hands when **Sam Loxton** pulled straight to him. Another of that happy 1948 band led by Don Bradman, unbeaten throughout their tour of Britain, Sam was another whom I saw often in later years. Even when nearly blind he was coaching the youngsters and loudly holding forth at the Gabba or at his Queensland Gold Coast home. One of his pronouncements must suffice: "Batting helmets? We didn't even wear 'em at Tobruk!"

My seasons as a first-grade cricketer in Sydney brought contact with the likes of Bob Simpson, Alan Davidson, Jim de Courcy, Ian Craig, Grahame Thomas, Gordon Rorke, and **Jim Burke**, with the last-named chucking me out ("lbw") with his wobbly-elbow off-spin, then crawling to a disciplined century devoid of any leg glances because my inswing-bowling skipper parked me at leg slip. As for **de Courcy**, he was the only player in my years of grade cricket who voiced an unpleasant remark. We were under orders to take our time as a follow-on loomed, so I took ages to reach the middle. This little chap who had toured England with the 1953 Australians came across as a bit nasty, as much as anything because his false teeth had been removed and the fangs gave him a sinister look.

There is a footnote to the perky and apparently high-spirited Jim Burke. As he passed along the upper gangway of the M.A.Noble Stand at the Sydney ground, having just finished a broadcasting stint, I called out to check with him how slow was that notorious century of his in the Bombay Test back in

1956. He gave a flippant reply and was gone. Soon afterwards we learned that, beset by financial, marital and health worries, Jim had shot himself.

You learned the hard way in grade cricket, and I was forever grateful to former Test umpire **Herb Elphinston** for sidling over after one day's play and saying, "Young fella, I reckon your back foot was moving in the wrong direction when [Frank] Misson bowled you." Elphinston had been officiating in Ashes Test matches only a few years previously, so I was willing to take him seriously. There was just that simple remark – perhaps a long-ago parallel with Jonny Bairstow's perceived technical flaw in the slightly hideous (from England's point of view) Ashes series of 2013-14. I never backed away thereafter for the next 37 years as a player (or as a writer who felt protective towards this beautiful game).

One of my best friends was Northamptonshire's high-scoring little Australian left-hander **Jock Livingston**, who at least gets a mention in the O'Reilly essay here. Jock was a matchless raconteur, until he began his meal, at which point he fell completely silent until he'd finished eating. One of his favourite stories concerned his county captain Freddie Brown. Likable in many ways, Freddie, it has to be said, was a bit of a bully. One evening he slammed the dressing-room door and, more red-faced than usual, tore into his players for their poor fielding that afternoon. When he'd finished, Jock, who had been sitting quietly in the corner, spoke up: "Excuse me, Mr Brown, but am I included in this criticism?" His captain thought hard: no, as usual Jock had fielded impeccably and given his all in the field, and did not deserve to be among those under attack. Years later I had some pleasant moments with **Freddie Brown**, that English bulldog cricketer, and always the vision of his heroics under Sydney's unforgiving sun in 1951 was sort of back-projected.

Another Australian exile was **John McMahon**, a left-arm spinner and (wounded) veteran of the battle of El Alamein. He had left Surrey when Tony Lock was preferred, and started again with Somerset. Liked a pint, did Johnny Mac, and he wrote engagingly about his contemporaries, essays I was very glad to use in *Wisden Cricket Monthly*. In a fun match at The Oval I once faced him, and his chinaman (wrong'un) was still operational. He was as sweet a man as I've ever encountered, though there seemed to be a strand of sadness running through his soul. My dealings with **Tony Lock** were brief: we were once on a television programme together, and he struck me as – how does one put it? – a bit strange?

Another close friend was **Ernie Toovey**, the Queensland left-hander of the 1950s, who may have been unique in having hit mystery bowler Jack Iverson for six in a Sheffield Shield match. Ernie was kind and thoughtful, placing books and ephemera aside for whenever we next met. The terrible shadows of his time as a prisoner-of-war in Changi, after HMAS Perth was sunk, never receded, and when one winter we flew to Queensland aboard a Japanese airliner I dared not tell him.

Arthur Chipperfield, who scored 99 on his Test debut, was also excellent company, both at home in Sydney (where he pulled from the wardrobe his proudest memento, a fading Durban newspaper placard proclaiming his 1935 Test century) and at Lord's, when we next bumped into each other. So cold were the conditions, the poor chap was lost under a heavy overcoat, scarf covering mouth. Not much prospect there of a tape-recorded interview, though it was amusing to hear his recall of being 99 not out at lunch against England in that Test at Trent Bridge in 1934, a bundle of nerves, unable to eat anything during the interval as he sat in a corner, then miserably falling to Ken Farnes, caught by 'keeper Ames three balls into resumption of play without adding to his score.

I'd like to have spent time with the rebellious **Sid Barnes** (Test batting average for Australia of 63), but a pen signature in my little book (he must have left his rubber stamp and ink-pad at home that day) was all that I managed. He always seemed to be a man on the move, but I do recall how curiously high-pitched and soft was this tough-guy spiv's voice.

Of more recent vintage, **David Hookes**, who was to be fatally injured in a street brawl in Melbourne one terrible night in 2004, was only 22 when he toured England in 1977, and I used to sit with him as he played the jukebox in the team's hotel. The link was some 1950s/1960s pop music, his liking for which both delighted and bemused me. In later years, when he became a broadcaster, I sometimes did a radio piece with him. "Well, Frithy, what's this book then? Must be about your 500th, eh?" he would bellow.

A near-contemporary of Hookesy was **Terry Jenner**, who recovered so inspirationally after a jail sentence for embezzlement and later helped Shane Warne to reach his apogee. My last brief encounter with Terry was at Adelaide Oval during the 2006-07 "whitewash" Ashes series. His wife, he said, had just bought a secondhand copy of my book *The Slow Men*, expecting that her husband might feature in it. He did. But not to TJ's complete liking.

Reference to the high trajectory of his leggers was taken the wrong way, and for a minute or so I thought he was going to land one on me. I was extremely sad that it ended like that.

There have been so many other encounters which don't quite warrant a capital E. One night, in a house in Brixton, I was among a small gathering invited to hear **C.L.R.James** speak. In a rasping, high-pitched, monotone voice the celebrated old Trinidadian, white-haired and well over six feet in height, spoke for some time about cricket and (mainly) politics. Later there was a brief conversation and he signed some books for me. No full-blooded Encounter there, but I was very pleased to have met this legendary character, whose book *Beyond a Boundary* is often referred to as the finest of all cricket books – not least by people who have never read it.

In 1971, I sought out **Victor Trumper's son**, who had played some first-class cricket as a fast bowler. It was a somewhat low-key meeting, and I recall that Vic junior had very few of his father's possessions. That same day, and less than a mile away, I found cricketer/writer/broadcaster **A.G. "Johnnie" Moyes's** widow, who kindly gave me one of his books, spoke of the pain he suffered for the rest of his life after wounds in the First World War, and then asked me to join her in a prayer before I departed.

While in the neighbourhood, I knocked on **Ernie Toshack's** door. He had been a brilliant left-arm medium-pacer in the 1940s, a tall, black-haired man, who had recently had a bit of trouble with the law after reels of wire had allegedly been taken from the railways. Ernie, with a crinkly smile, had touchingly worn his Australian blazer in court, and Keith Miller had given a character reference. Now he and his wife Cathleen invited me in, produced tea and cake for a stranger, and dragged out the old scrapbooks.

Around that time I found myself with **Frank Buckle**, who had been a club-mate and friend of "Tibby" Cotter, the hostile Australian fast bowler who was killed in 1917 at Beersheba. Frank had a shattered stump at home, a precious Cotter relic, and said I could have it, but the handover never took place. At least I had been a handshake away from wild colonial boy Cotter.

There were so many other cricketers who, with a few more meetings, might have made it into this series. **"Gubby" Allen** was a major near-miss. I saw him at many functions, but only once got talking to him seriously. The exchange bordered on the farcical. Even all those years ago I was unknowingly preparing to write a book some day on the Bodyline Test series of 1932-33.

G.O.Allen listened to my opening remarks before placing his fingers on my forearm and assuring me that Bodyline didn't begin until the *third* Test, at Adelaide. Now this ran counter to all documented history. Bradman had been bombarded even before the Tests began. So had Fingleton. How could Gubby possibly say such a thing? Then came the somewhat predictable (attempted) clincher: "My dear chap, I was *there!*" And so he may have been. But where, from his usual short-leg position, had he been looking during those earlier matches, including the opener at Sydney when Stan McCabe's heroism midst the assault brought him 187 runs, mostly from crisp and often lucky hooks and pulls?

At least, while spending some time with India's Test veterans, a cherished handshake with the aged **Lala Amarnath** was followed by a brief utterance which was delivered in such a soft voice that I failed to grasp its substance: so there was to be no controversy there, even though Amarnath was one of the most controversial cricketers of them all.

It's amusing to recall an evening at a Sheffield Cricket Lovers Society dinner as co-speaker with **Norman Yardley**, who captained England in Bradman's last few Tests. The prime item that survives in the memory bank of that evening's conversation was Norman's remark to my wife: that she had nice legs. It made a change from the stuffy chat that stultifies many a cricket gathering.

Acquaintance with **F.G.Mann** left one perplexing memory: how could such a charming and urbane man, with the Test captaincy and high office in cricket as well as an eminent position in business and a superb war record, be so tense before addressing a press conference? Maybe it was because of the nature of the announcement that George had to make: bad news for South Africa, with which he had cricket and marital connections: sanctions against their cricketers were to be intensified.

His contemporary, **S.C."Billy"Griffith**, was another to be much admired, not only for his distinguished war service but for the calm way he cleared a packed Lord's ground one lovely August afternoon in 1973. His loud-speaker announcement informed us all that there had been a bomb threat. I was the first one out of the press-box, and down the staircase in a flash. I'd found Billy most helpful when the 1970 England v Rest of the World matches were being referred to as "Test matches". In response to my enquiry he went to a drawer and pulled out the original ICC definition of a Test match (which was stated to be exclusively a match between two full member countries of the ICC). The

1970 contests had been nothing more than a commercial expedient following cancellation of the scheduled tour by South Africa, though it took *Wisden* and others some time to grasp the fact. That 2014 sees Billy's centenary comes as a surprise. He would have been somewhat disgusted at the modern ICC's playing fast and loose with that definition 35 years later with that futile "Test" match in Melbourne between Australia and a World XI.

In the 1960s some of the speakers at Cricket Society gatherings in London were worth travelling many miles to see and hear. One such was Canon **Jack Parsons**, who had been driven all the way up from Cornwall by the cricket bookseller **Ted Brown** (from whom I acquired many good cricket items over the years). A remarkable old gentleman, one of the most powerful hitters the game has known, Parsons had been both an amateur and a professional with Warwickshire, and had served in the First World War. How the names from way back echoed around the room that evening as we listened to a voice truly from the long-ago. This man had taken part in the cavalry charge at Huj, in Palestine in 1917, the last such full-scale operation in British military history. After that, belting a half-volley over the Edgbaston pavilion was a fairly simple task.

Though they probably think otherwise, what dull lives modern cricketers lead.

Another Great War survivor with whom I had contact – though not in the flesh – was that English literary and broadcasting eminence **J.B.Priestley**, whom I approached by letter with a request for a foreword to a book I was writing on cricket's "Golden Age" (1890-1914). The legendary, grumpy Yorkshireman agreed to write it, but became impatient when the manuscript was slow in reaching him. In a follow-up letter he threatened to drop the idea if I didn't hurry up. I got the typescript to him eventually, and was gratified to receive a powerful foreword soon afterwards, made all the more feelingful for his having endured the horrors of the Great War. He served in the Duke of Wellington's Regiment, and was wounded twice and saw many pals killed. As for a fee, the great man came up with a simple solution: a box of fine Havana cigars to be left on his doorstep.

Early in the 1970s I passed a privileged hour or so with **Aidan Crawley**, who was then MCC president. He bought me a beer and there was a cordial chat about this and that before the formalities began, the occasion being the unveiling of the Bradman painting (by Hannaford) in the Long Room at Lord's.

It was also the first time I met Lady Bradman. Jessie was as charming as a lady could be, and the event was truly top-shelf, if all too brief. Crawley had been a big-hitting batsman for Oxford and Kent, a top television executive, an MP firstly in the Labour ranks and then Conservative, but most impressive by far was his series of bold escapes from German prisoner-of-war camps after being shot down in North Africa. A strong-jawed man of rare distinction, a most remarkable Englishman, he called his autobiography *Leap Before You Look*. Some of us may do this some of the time. The wondrous but modest A.M.Crawley seems to have done it repeatedly.

Another welcome but brief interlude was with gentle **Jack Ikin**, and it led inevitably to the question of his "catch" off Bradman in the gully in the 1946 Brisbane Test, one of the most famous controversies in Ashes history. Jack had no doubt at all about the legitimacy of the catch. Notwithstanding England's disappointment (and Wally Hammond's lurid utterance of outrage) Bradman's survival at 28 and advance to 187 altered the shape of post-war cricket, and greatly to its benefit.

Further insight into the Bradman legend came not through a personal meeting but in a letter: to **Allan Watkins**, who had the best view (from silly mid-off) when the Don played that final Test innings at The Oval in 1948. After the rousing reception from spectators and the England players, did the legendary Australian have tears in his eyes? Not at all, asserted Allan. (And in a simple and innocent cricket era, when the business of statistics was unsophisticated and given little attention, the world was *not* instantly hopping around in near-hysteria at Bradman's missing out on a Test average of 100. In fact it took some time before the public became aware.)

Letters, of course, provide further insights into cricketers' make-up. I have built up a collection of over 6000, starting with a reply from **Jack Hobbs** back in 1958. In his kindly fashion he wrote that he hoped that Australia's latest batting discovery, Norm O'Neill, wouldn't turn out to be a "second Bradman" since Bradman was far too good. You can tell much from handwriting, the type of paper used, and the style of letterhead. Each communication is a kind of encounter. Even small details can be useful: **Herby Taylor**, who tamed S.F.Barnes in 1913-14 and was for years considered the best of all South Africa's batsmen, signed his abbreviated christian name with that final "y" and not "ie": proof positive if ever it were needed. The autocratic pre-war Yorkshire captain **Brian Sellers** had on his letterhead a sketch of a couple making love. **Keith**

Miller wrote completely unconventionally, seldom using the introductory "Dear" and sometimes awarding recipients OBEs they hadn't earned. **W.W. "Billy" Wade**, the South Africa wicketkeeper, and once a prisoner-of-war, wrote some fascinating letters. But then to dip into a letter collection of this magnitude would be to produce a book much larger than this one.

In quite another context, I think of **Arthur McIntyre**, the dexterous Surrey and sometime England wicketkeeper. I was listening to the wireless commentary when he was run out while attempting a third run during a crisis in the Brisbane thriller of 1950-51. A quarter of a century later, as head coach at The Oval, he branded my elder son as a chucker. Thanks, Arthur. He was bordering on fury in the dressing-room during a Surrey 2nd XI match when he saw how worn and unpolished the ball was after we'd bowled with it for 45 overs. As captain, I copped the worst of the blast. In this match, incidentally, we fielded a four-man pace attack (Bob Lowe, Andy Mack, David Smith, and Otto Verrinder) years before Clive Lloyd dreamed up the idea. It is stressed that we bowled no more than one or two bouncers an over.

Some of McIntyre's Surrey triumphs in the 1950s came under the leadership of **Stuart Surridge**, a strong man if ever there was one. In 1964, my first summer of English club cricket, I had the pleasure of being dismissed (Cheam v MCC) c E.A.Bedser b Surridge. As we all sat on stools at the bar that evening, Surridge asked if I'd ever been to The Oval, and would I like a ticket for the forthcoming Test match? I leapt at the chance. Two days later the ticket arrived – complete with invoice.

The cricket societies up and down the country have afforded great pleasure in the gatherings among like-minded souls. Only once, in 1977 at Brighton, did things turn dodgy. At question time I was asked the burning question of the hour: what did I think about the new Packer intrusion and Tony Greig's role? Greig, of course, was Sussex captain, and a throbbing sense of betrayal had descended over the county. I tried to analyse the situation, asking if perhaps some good could come of it, with cricketers' remuneration likely to improve. I felt the room freezing over, the members scowling, some even shaking their heads. To the rescue came the president, **George Cox**, the genial former Sussex batsman, who tried to reason with his patently unhappy members. I was grateful for George's effort, which may have saved me from a lynching, but changed the membership's view not one jot. It was a mighty relief to be asked back to Brighton some years later – by which time we all knew how the

Packer revolution had turned the beloved game into a garish and cash-laden branch of show business.

I once asked **Jack Young**, the Middlesex and England left-arm spinner, to write an article for *Wisden Cricket Monthly*, and he took it very seriously indeed, insisting that he should get on a train and bring it to me personally. I'm glad he did, because he was a charming little man, full of fun, in a kind of contradiction of his feat of bowling 14 consecutive maiden overs for Middlesex against Gloucestershire at Bristol in 1949. I admired his stoicism, for he was clearly in pain and used a stick when walking.

It was a thrill to stand alongside **Arthur Milton** in the slips in a charity match. This easy-going double international from Bristol was grace and elegance personified. As Harold Rhodes whisked one bouncer after another past batsmen's noses, Arthur murmured: "Rather them than me!" He was no doubt being modest. He could handle most situations in his undemonstrative way.

It was immensely gratifying that same day not only to face the bowling of the shrewd little off-spinner **Fred Titmus** (while recalling the sight of him taking 7 for 79 in the Sydney Test way back in 1962-63) and being caught on the midwicket boundary off him, but surviving a precious couple of overs from **Basil D'Oliveira**, whose place in history is as far more than a notable cricketer. It was such a memorable day for me, for I also batted with **Reg Simpson**, whose 156 not out at Melbourne in 1951 set up England's first post-war victory against Australia, most of it listened to on the wireless in Sydney. Now aged 62 and with a comfortable paunch, Reg batted as serenely as ever. And every summer, during Trent Bridge Test matches, he was also good for an insightful conversation. It's neither normal nor desirable to stand talking to a chap while wondering if one day you'll be writing his obituary. If such a thought did intrude during those conversations it would have been coupled with the fervent hope that the necessity would arise many, many years later: as it eventually did.

Not so long ago I offered perhaps the longest-delayed congratulations any cricketer has ever received. **Roy Tattersall**, brilliant offspinner, negligible batsman, had managed to hang on as England's No.11 at Melbourne while 74 precious runs were added, Reg Simpson finishing with that famous 156 not out. Now, over half-a-century later and at a Wisden dinner, I impulsively seized the chance to grasp the slightly bemused "Tatt's" hand and thank him for his effort so long ago at the MCG, closing the circle in a manner of speaking.

Playing in "Press Tests" meant rubbing shoulders with some top cricketers. There was the elegant wicketkeeper **Keith Andrew**, a good conversationalist and thoroughly decent man who believed in courtesy, something seldom found in his noisy fraternity. (I'll never be really sure that he picked my wrong'un either: surely must have, having read the wondrous George Tribe's wrist variety so beautifully in Northants matches back in the 1950s.) **Graham Roope** played with us once or twice, and was also very solicitous. Such a glorious slip fieldsman was he that when he seemed to have floored a slip catch off Botham's bowling in a Lord's Test, I was moved to pop down to the England dressing-room to verify the aberration, such was our sense of disbelief. **Eddie Barlow**, the powerhouse South African all-rounder, played with us once and, spotting faults all round, made it his duty to suggest this and that, always in the most kindly and constructive fashion. I couldn't help reflecting on "Bunter" at his ebullient best, sleeves rolled up almost to the armpits, bowling flat out at Sydney in 1964, looking fit to burst. **Bob Woolmer** was another courteous individual, notably thoughtful too. He loved talking theory, and his mysterious death in Jamaica in 2007 still leaves troublesome echoes.

Another who died far too young was **Graham Dilley**. As a youthful newcomer in the England dressing-room in Melbourne in 1979-80 he seemed bored, so we had a miniature contest in a spare corner of the room, and it was good fun teasing him from ten yards away. Soon afterwards I encountered him in the hotel bar, propped on a stool, wires trailing from his neck. After the Frankenstein jokes, he revealed that it was the latest treatment for muscle problems. "Hello, Mr Editor!" was his stock greeting, to which I would reply "Hello, Mr Medium-pacer!" His death at 52 stunned the cricket world.

Tragedy cannot be quantified, but it's possible that the most tragic case since the Second World War was the death of **Ben Hollioake** in a car accident in March 2002, in Perth, when he was only 24. He was not only a rapturously gifted cricketer: he was the most charming and easy-going of young men. He and brother Adam played in a Bunburys match at Ripley shortly before Ben died, and during our pre-match conversation his charm and ethereal nature radiated – as later did his powerful arm. A long throw from Ben almost tore the rubber from the palms of the gloves. A close-up later of his smiling batsmanship completed the day, one which became hallowed in memory.

Yet another whose early death shocked and saddened the cricket community was **Malcolm Marshall**, possibly the most effective of the West Indies fast-bowling terrorisers. I'd had a quick drink with him one evening at the team hotel during a northern Test match, but didn't get to talk to him seriously until a charity match in Hampshire soon after his retirement. I embarked on a calm and serious discussion with him about fast-bowling violence and about my journalistic protests and the backlash. He listened sympathetically and gave every indication of being willing to talk it over reasonably. This was the moment I'd been waiting for, a "scientific" analysis of this touchy subject. Then he was called to the phone, and we had to take the field, and that was that. Not, I suppose, that he was likely to repent on behalf of his bouncer-happy brotherhood for the dozens of batsmen sent to hospital during those years of excessive hostility. But his thoughts now that the battles were history would have been of interest.

In a charity match in the 1980s I had to contend with **Don Brennan** of Yorkshire and England behind the stumps. It was another revelation. He chattered and waffled and irritated non-stop. Around that time this scourge of mouthy keepers and close fielders was on the increase at all levels of the game, although I don't suppose the blame can be pinned solely on Brennan. Another Yorkshireman, **Don Wilson**, was also never short of an ebullient word. He came as an "escort" on one of our Wisden tours, but when Elton John and entourage arrived unexpectedly and took over one entire floor at our Sydney hotel, we had a big rehousing problem to deal with. The tour party needed to be calmed, reassured and reorganised. So where was Don? His response had been to lock himself in his room with his wife, drinking champagne, the cure for most problems.

I found **Mike Denness** very agreeable company. A polished individual, he was perfectly suited to the PR work he carried out after his Test days had ended. I managed to forgive him for breaking my 19th Century hero Drewy Stoddart's record for the highest score by an England captain in Australia. And I regretted the occasion when someone at a reception asked me what Denness's career amounted to, and my reply (along the lines that it ended rather bluntly and shambolically after he put Australia in at Edgbaston in 1975 and lost by an innings) was delivered without knowing that Mike was right behind us and within earshot. Perhaps he'd heard it all so many times before. I last saw him at Alec Bedser's funeral.

A highly unusual brief encounter took place at a reception at Lord's in 1997, when I was thrilled to meet **W.G.Grace's** last surviving grandchild, 92-year-old **Mrs Primrose Worthington**, a tall and charming lady who spoke of sitting on grandfather's knee and plucking strands from his famous beard. It matched meeting **F.R.Spofforth's** grand-daughters some years earlier when they lived in Guildford: less frustrating than meeting **W.L.Murdoch's** grandson, who unfortunately was deaf. The good fortune of meeting Golden Age fast bowler **Tom Richardson's** son in the 1960s led to the acquisition of two balls (mounted) used by the great man in Surrey and England matches in the 1890s.

Of course, I've known numerous cricket writers and broadcasters, and it was fascinating to discover what sort of people they really were: the ultra-serious **J.M.Kilburn** from Yorkshire; the somewhat grim **John Kay** from up North; **Tom Goodman**, the gentleman journo from the *Sydney Morning Herald*; the high-powered award-winning **Ian Wooldridge,** whose encounters ranged from Joe Louis to Idi Amin; **Peter West**, master of the friendly scowl, smooth and professional, possessed of a disciplined voice the like of which is seldom if ever heard nowadays. Only late in his life did I learn that **Alex Bannister**, a trusted cricket writer, was in action in the bloody conflict at Anzio, where his best friend was shot dead in the trench beside him. The keen little Yorkshire-born veteran photographer **Ken Kelly** was another Anzio survivor, but he could never speak about it, tears welling at the very thought of it. How very different were the writers and photographers of those few decades following the Second World War: a special breed whose successors were bound to be of a much different hue.

Reg Hayter ran a flourishing media agency through which almost every post-war British newspaper writer had passed as a youngster, and in the mid-1960s I was just one of his "proteges", writing brief reports from football and rugby matches for a pittance, and hoping for a break. Reg set up my first book, a ghosted job with John Edrich, which was published the day that man landed on the Moon, something I chose to take as a propitious omen. I did a bit of this and that, sometimes overseen by **Chris Lander**, a thrusting, laughing young journalist who was on his way to one of the highest-paid jobs, cricket correspondent of *The Sun*, but not destined for a long life. My assignments included ringing through running reports from the southern Test matches, mainly for two old-timers from the Midlands, **John Solan** and **W.G. "Bill" Wanklyn**, pleasant men both of them. Some years later, when I found myself stripped of the editorship of *The Cricketer*, proprietor **Ben Brocklehurst** called in the Hayter agency to take over. The first issue under the new regime was blistered by around 100 errors, starting with a 36-point mis-spelling on the front cover, cold comfort for this desperate ex-editor out in the wilderness.

Early attempts to get something into *The Cricketer* magazine in the mid-1960s had led me to travel down the A3 to Cobham to meet **Arthur Langford**, who had been Plum Warner's right-hand man through most of the magazine's existence. Arthur was something of a legend, having, with his wife, kept the magazine going through the difficulties of the war years. But he was not now very encouraging. So all those years of frustrated endeavour were actually creating for me a build-up of energy which, when finally released, saw me working around the clock for many years and well past normal retirement age.

Some readers will be familiar with the writings of **G.D.Martineau**, whose essays appeared in *The Cricketer* and in a couple of delectable little books. He also penned verse. When driving to the West Country in the 1970s I decided to chance calling in to see him in Lyme Regis. Gerard Durani Martineau received me graciously and signed some books, but he was clearly ailing, and died shortly afterwards. I later discovered that he too was a First World War veteran.

When it came to broadcasting, there has never been a finer cricket commentator than **Alan McGilvray**, except that he was rather short on humour, and enjoyed nothing more than having a crack at Don Bradman. Somewhere Don had rubbed him the wrong way, and Alan, in that extraordinarily agreeable and confidential voice, would recall gleefully how he and his fast bowler Lincoln Hynes plotted DGB's dismissal for a duck in a Sheffield Shield match at Sydney in 1936. This recital came at the launch party for Alan's book – the only launch I've ever attended where there were no books. They simply hadn't turned up. Earlier, Alan had chipped batsman Craig Serjeant for not wearing a tie, saying it was unbecoming of a possible future Australian Test captain. "Yes," coolly replied the young batsman, "but I'm not captain yet, Macca."

The complexities of relationships make for fascinating reflection. Cricket inspires firm friendships, but professional rivalry brings out the worst in some of them. John Arlott was not always comfortable following McGilvray on commentary, aware as he was of the Australian's deeper, instinctive understanding of the technical nuances. This seemed to debar true friendship (and even to lead to subversive altering of broadcasting schedules), and they were said to have actively disliked each other. So it may be imagined how stunned I was one day when I arrived at The Old Sun in Alresford to find Alan sitting in an armchair in John's parlour.

The name **Howard Marshall** would mean little to most cricket-lovers of today, but he had the most smooth and appealing voice of all when it came to cricket commentary. He worked in an age when good voice quality was a pre-requisite for broadcasting. Today anything goes, from the BBC's "screeching sheilas" to the guttural and illiterate voices which assail us from countless television and radio stations. In the 1930s Marshall was the Voice of Cricket on the wireless, heroically performing without the support of scorer or fellow commentators. His description of Hedley Verity's spin destruction of Australia in the 1934 Lord's Test match is one of cricket's archive gems. But by 1972, when I wrote to him, he explained in his courteous reply that he was too frail to compose an article, though he expressed "pleasure at being remembered". He died soon afterwards.

Dear old **Ray Robinson**, the scrupulous observer, researcher and expressive writer, was another gentleman of the press-box, a kind, thoughtful and generous chap, meticulous researcher and witty writer, bent low over his notepad as his sight deteriorated. The Australian cricketers either side of the Second World War liked him and trusted him. In today's harsh, deadly serious and sometimes bitter climate, most cricket journalists are deprived of that kind of friendship. One of Ray's claims to fame was the coining of the word "Bodyline" when, as a sub-editor, he worked on Hugh Buggy's match report in 1932-33.

Another who was trusted by the players all those years ago was the last surviving cricket correspondent from the stormy Bodyline Test series, **Gilbert Mant**. He preserved a fund of stories, one of which posed a very awkward dilemma for me: should I include it in my book *Bodyline Autopsy*? It was an apparently watertight case against Don Bradman as the chap who leaked the outburst by Australia's captain Bill Woodfull in the direction of England's manager Plum Warner during the Adelaide Test match of 1932-33. I endeavoured to turn the revelation, bequeathed to me by Gilbert, to good purpose, believing that the highly respected Australian captain's words served the cause well in that it now allowed the Australian public at large to understand that even he, Bill Woodfull, deeply resented Bodyline. The undecided and the hesitant were now free to give full vent to their own outrage.

Another of Gilbert Mant's stories was more amusing. Did Wally Hammond fall to a full-toss from leg-spinner Bradman in that same 1933 Adelaide Test? Everyone in the press-box was curious to know, and as Reuters' correspondent, Mant, who knew Hammond fairly well, was just the chap to ask him. So he popped his head into the England dressing-room and called out: "Wally! Was that a full-toss?" The response was splattered with five-star expletives. Gilbert returned to the press-box and calmly announced: "Wally confirms that it was indeed a full-toss." It was an inspiration to see *three* books come from the Mant typewriter – one of them about the fall of Singapore in 1942 (he was there) – when the man was in his nineties.

Then there was the industrious **Jack Pollard**. A little dynamo of a man, he advised me to try my luck in journalism back in my native land, England. So my young family and I joined the exodus from Australia in the steady convoy of passenger ships (which sometimes rocked alarmingly) in the early 1960s, following the likes of Frank Ifield, Germaine Greer, Rolf Harris, Clive James, and The Seekers up the English Channel. Some years later, as we exchanged airletters and pictures and text, Pollard became spiky and tiresome. Unfortunately, the only language he knew was his books' sales figures. The lesson, I think, was that one had to work hard at growing old gracefully, and to allow that the newcomers are entitled to their sometimes noisy years of "glory".

I once sat close to **Louis Duffus** in the Lord's press-box near the end of his career. He was Sydney-born but for some years South Africa's premier writer. There was, too, the outrageous **R.S. Whitington**: Dick was many times married, loved a drink and a laugh, but never let facts obstruct a good story. An unavoidably stern review of one of his later careless effusions drew a furious response from Dick, and that was that.

Frustrating in another sense was being only very briefly close to **Lindsay Hassett**, the amusing little Australian Test captain. How I wish I'd engineered a chat in depth with him concerning his pre-war Victoria contemporary Ross Gregory, except that I was with Lindsay so long ago that I could not have known then that some time in the future I would acquire Ross's wartime diary and write a book on his cricket career and tragic death while serving

29

with the RAAF as a Wellington navigator in India in 1942. Hassett, with his surprisingly deep voice, was one of the most humorous of cricketers, and is usually unjustly overlooked today when the best are being discussed. I'm left to treasure walking with him across the Moore Park car park outside the Sydney Cricket Ground, and also chatting aimlessly at an airport in South Africa. Years earlier, as a teenager, I thought his signature, collected outside the SCG pavilion, was just about the most elegant of them all. His prolific and stylish batting, not least the late cut, wasn't bad either.

Ben Barnett, Australia's pre-war wicketkeeper, was another who would have had some interesting personal memories of Ross Gregory, but this was, alas, all out of sequence. Ben had been a prisoner of the Japanese during the Second World War, but naturally never spoke of the dreadful experience except to intimates. Having settled for some years in England, he was often to be seen at the Test matches, and came across as the most amiable of men. History has probably treated him badly in that he is "credited" with missing a stumping when Len Hutton was about 40 and on his way to 364 at The Oval in 1938. I recently read that it was an extremely difficult miss, with Hutton going through with a heave and getting his bat back fast. Just how difficult was it, Ben? I missed my chance.

Yet another war veteran was **Bob Cristofani**, who played in the 1945 Victory "Tests" and was a St George player. I'd netted with Bob at Hurstville as a St George colt in the 1950s, and was surprised to see him bring his own new ball along for the practice sessions. He was a zealous theorist, and I recall sitting next to him at a St George club dinner and discussing what precisely was a "half cock" stroke. Years later, settled in England, he vigorously preached the virtue of standing a yard out of the crease when facing the likes of Waqar Younis and Wasim Akram. Dismissing the risk to teeth and cheekbones, Bob believed that the late swing would be countered and the bowlers would be confused. I interviewed Bob for the Imperial War Museum sound archive. His story ended most poignantly when he described seeing his best mate shot out of the sky in front of him.

Another RAAF veteran was **Ross Stanford**, who flew on 47 operations over Europe as a Lancaster pilot, a DFC winner with 417 Squadron. He had been so nervous when he first batted with Don Bradman for South Australia that he ran himself out. He'd shown his promise as a 14-year-old by scoring 416 not out in a school match, but was equally talented at party songs, ever ready to sing *Along Came a Bloody Blackbird*, a ditty that had amused the rich English ladies during the war. Ross reckoned that they jingled their jewellery as the Aussie airmen sang with gusto. The last time I spoke to Ross was by phone, and he was chuckling at the fact that so problematic was his health now that he was compelled to wear a nappy. Brave, cheerful, tough fellow, typical of his generation.

Elsewhere in the world of music, in the course of putting a video programme together (*Benson & Hedges Golden Greats: Batsmen*) I decided to incorporate the song *Our Don Bradman*. This meant approaching the music publishers, and they in turn referred me to the writer himself, the fabled **Jack O'Hagan**. I was surprised that he was still alive, but during a long telephone call he came across as the most kindly of men. His *Road to Gundagai* is just as well-known and cherished as the bouncy Bradman song, and to my astonishment old Jack said we could use the Bradman tune for nothing. He just seemed pleased to be remembered and consulted. (The publishers, alas, were to take a more businesslike approach.)

I think back to other journalistic, even poetic, profiles. **Alan Ross**, veteran of the ghastly Arctic convoys in the Second World War and much admired writer on cricket and other things, was always friendly disposed, sometimes, I suspected from a chance swivel sighting at a reception, potentially almost too much so.

Thinking of poets, I once wrote to **John Betjeman** asking him if he'd care to review John Snow's little book of verse, but he declined – ever so politely, of course – saying that he never reviewed living authors. There was a sweet postscript: "I am very glad to have a letter on your writing paper [*Wisden Cricket Monthly*] and shall flourish it about."

It was a pleasure to deal with the then leading New Zealand cricket writer **R.T. "Dick" Brittenden**, who was also an ex-Serviceman. When touring his beautiful country I was invited to his golf day at Waitikiri, and he proved to be a perfect host, displaying extraordinary patience as I tried to hack my way out of the exotic ferns and bushes in the rough.

Elsewhere, the Anglo-Indian **Dicky Rutnagur**, who died in 2013, was a sweet-natured and somewhat fragile man, good to have around. He rang me one evening to say that he'd just finished reading my book on Archie Jackson, and hadn't been able to stop weeping, poor fellow. It was hard to know what to say to that. Then there was **Jim Coldham**, editor of *The Cricket Society*

Journal, a veteran of the dreadful Burma campaign in the Second World War, a supportive chap who hedged his bets when *Wisden Cricket Monthly* started up in 1979, since he didn't want to upset his friends at *The Cricketer*.

Rex Alston, the immediate-post-war cricket commentator with the crispest voice of all, was a cordial man and a good host at his home near Dorking, where visitors were invited to sign their names on a wall. Rex knew the value of occasional silence when describing cricket on air. This is now a lost art. Another of that generation, all but forgotten now, was **Michael Melford**, once an elite athlete and a soldier, sound and reliable as a cricket writer and one whose dignified behaviour I often recall in the press-box when things get slightly rowdy. **Norman de Mesquita** was yet another very agreeable fellow, who brought his own brand of joviality to the gathering.

Another to die far too early was **Bill Frindall**, statistician and businessman, a chap who took himself very seriously, particularly when bowling his "fast" stuff – which naturally rendered it especially rewarding to take runs off him in press matches. Then there was **Alan Gibson**, the acerbic, cerebral broadcaster whose articulate delivery left the others, apart from John Arlott and Don Mosey, well behind. Drink got to Alan in the end, but he could be very funny, as well as very cutting. I had a brief but sharp exchange with him near the end. Fire with fire?

It's been so very sad to see them all depart for the Great Pavilion. I vividly recall strolling through Melbourne's Yarra Park with **John Thicknesse** one Test match evening when the apparently carefree, somewhat cynical, thick-skinned gambler and evening newspaper cricket writer, suddenly uttered a heart-felt lament – it seemed so uncharacteristic – that with retirement now imminent he was going to miss Australia terribly after seven tours. Not all that long afterwards "Thickers" was dead. I miss **Richard Streeton** too. Dick was an old-fashioned, square-jawed cricket and rugby journalist, author of an admirable biography of Percy Fender, and fondly nicknamed "Hawkins" after the ever-heroic Jack Hawkins of stage and screen. An abiding image of Dick is of his stoic stance when suffering from long-term "Delhi belly" on the 1984-85 tour of India. We were all sitting in a group one evening at **Venkataraghavan's** house when I spotted Dick's large overnight bag. What on earth did he want with that here? The stark truth was that it was full of toilet rolls.

Another whose friendship I initially enjoyed, from as long ago as 1967, was **Christopher Martin-Jenkins**. Magazine competition was principally responsible for curdling it. He was for a time editor of *The Cricketer* while I ran its new rival, my own *Wisden Cricket Monthly*. Later, he and his acolytes, resenting *WCM's* success, did their best to undermine me. Possessed of a voice made for broadcasting, but an unexceptional writer, he was always careful to display his shiny side. However, through a series of incidents he revealed a less attractive side to me. Two samples must suffice. **Don Mosey** of Test Match Special was an articulate broadcaster, who rejoiced in referring to his TMS producer as "the tea boy" and once had us reaching for dictionaries when he dubbed David Gower "otiose". Don invited me to record a goodwill message for the dying Neil Hawke over in Adelaide. As I emerged misty-eyed from the darkness of the BBC caravan, there at the bottom of the steps was CMJ. "What are *you* doing here?" he barked. His mask had slipped, not for the first time. As for his autobiography, published shortly before his death in January 2013, he penned some spiteful untruths concerning my editorship of *The Cricketer* in the 1970s. It was a gratuitous slap. Yet in one way it was a relief to see, out in the open, the long-running subversion, which also infected Cricket Writers Club business. He would certainly have known that I did not walk out on *The Cricketer* in 1978. Mr Brocklehurst pushed me overboard. As for my expenses: there weren't any, in contrast to my successor's cushy number. I considered legal action over his published denigration, but it was known that he was seriously ill, so I left it. Maybe he had the last laugh; maybe not. I was sad that the original friendship all those many years ago had long since curdled. Aside from the slurs, he wrote that I was "stubborn and punctilious, a perfectionist", a description that, as an editor, researcher and writer, I accept with pride. I also accept that I am "inclined to be free with his [my] criticism of others", for the opposite to this is to be secretive and to back-stab. I've had more than enough of that. What's paramount is that my highly-valued friends know who they are.

Mention of the mighty **Neil Hawke** reminds me of a happier time, when the big fella nursed me through my 40th birthday at a bar in Melbourne, thus sealing a memorable day which had begun with breakfast with the Bradmans, Derek Randall having brought to life the main event – the Centenary Test – by moving halfway to his unforgettable 174 that afternoon.

There was no more cantankerous writer and researcher than **Irving Rosenwater**. In the 1960s he was a regular friend, enthusiastic and encouraging, interesting to know, if you were prepared to accept his never less than dogmatic views, theatrically loud voice, and noisy eating. This man pursued perfection, and he paraded his scholarship volubly, presenting himself as completely perfect. He was unquestionably as well informed on cricket history and statistics as anyone, but his lack of both tolerance and humour made him difficult company, and as the years passed he became even more uncomfortable to be with. Unmarried and spiralling down a hole of his own making, he was all but friendless at the end. It was sad, but no-one else could be blamed.

There was a memorable encounter between "Rosie" and **Norman Preston**, who was not one of *Wisden's* outstanding editors, but a fascinating figure all the same with his Pickwickian shape and tendency to go very red in the face when stressed. His insistence on sticking (for years) to the inclusion of the 1970 Rest of the World XI contests in the Test match section lessened the respect that many had held towards him – and it also had Rosenwater shouting at him from the base of the staircase at The Oval and old Norman shouting back from the balcony. My own little attempted wind-up on Norman a year or two later didn't go down at all well: as I passed his seat in the press-box I flung open my shirt to reveal a Lillee-and-Thomson tee-shirt. Norman wasn't amused.

It was an infinitely more comfortable experience being with **Gerald Brodribb**, who wrote some deeply-researched cricket books but would be just as likely to take visitors off to see his Roman excavation in Sussex. He collected material relating to the 19th Century cricketer/artist Nicholas Wanostrocht ("Felix"), and promised to leave me an item or two in his will, but somehow I missed out. Never mind. At least I was able to buy a few items from **Crawford White**, the tall, suave and trim-moustached *Daily Express* writer and scoop-seeker, the David Niven of the press-box. He too is much missed.

Cricket is a form of escape from real life, a sanctuary, a cosy club with only sporadic friction. On the whole it attracts the best of people. To have spent well over half-a-century, mostly at the heart of it, is nearly all that a starry-eyed lad could have wanted. I've been recalling so many, but when it is too late I shall probably remember a few more, with anecdotes attached.

However, a confession is necessary here. Cricket apart, it was an altogether more profound experience, albeit on cricket occasions, to shake hands with RAF wartime heroes such as the most highly decorated bomber pilot of the Second World War, Group Captain (Lord) **Leonard Cheshire**, VC, OM, DFC,

DSO and two bars, and Group Captain (Sir) **Douglas Bader**, DSO, DFC, CBE, FRAeS, DL, truly great men both of them. I later wrote to Douglas Bader concerning his hurricane innings of 65 for the RAF in a first-class match at The Oval in 1931. It was surprising that in his reply he thought it necessary to tell me that he'd lost both legs in a pre-war flying accident. It seemed to me that this was as well-known a fact as WG's beard.

Very much earlier, at the age of nineteen, I had stood in a Royal Australian Air Force guard of honour for the heroic American flyer General **Jimmy Doolittle**, who had taken off from an aircraft carrier and led the daring bombing raid on Tokyo. How frustrating it was to have to remain at attention and not start up a conversation with the diminutive legend as he passed.

Earlier still, perched on my father's shoulders, I had seen the **King** and **Queen** and **Winston Churchill** and Field Marshal **Montgomery** from a distance in the VE Day parade in London in 1945. And in 1950, when in Canberra with the Air Training Corps, I had met the Air Minister, Sir **Thomas White**, DFC, who had been a First World War flying hero, escaping from Turkish captivity, and had married Prime Minister Deakin's daughter, and was now about to become Australia's High Commissioner in London. What rendered that encounter unforgettable was that the diminutive, white-haired Tommy White, a man of such distinction, somehow made all of us cadets seem so important to him. There was a cherished handshake.

There could, of course, have been nothing like that with the distant Churchill and "Monty". The next-best thing had been to name my two pet carp after them.

Many years later, at a Lord's Taverners dinner, came the chance to meet Rear Admiral **Tony Miers**, a naval Victoria Cross winner (submarines). A further cherished "wartime" handshake was with Lieutenant-General Sir **Oliver Leese**, KCB, CBE, DSO, who had been wounded three times in the First World War and was later one of Montgomery's key men in the North Africa campaign only to be sacked by Mountbatten when later serving in the Far East. (It happens to the best of them/us.) The treasured Leese handshake came when this then-young author received the inaugural Cricket Society Literary Award for the A.E.Stoddart biography, back in 1971.

The Stoddart book brings to mind a very lucky break in the late 1960s when my letter in the *Daily Telegraph*, asking for information from anyone who knew my hero (he died in 1915), brought forth a response from a man who was over 100 years of age. This was **Francis Cooke**, a yachting writer, who had been to the same school as "Stoddy" in the 1870s and had known him well. He remembered personal details that no other could have imparted, and, mercifully, his deafness proved no great barrier to communication. No personal encounter has delighted me more. Mr Cooke was the last remaining person on this planet who could have confirmed that the great "Stoddy's" voice bore a faint touch of his "Geordie" origins, and that he conveyed love notes between the future England cricket and rugby captain and a girl in the school. I drove fast to Essex to meet Mr Cooke, and slowly, deeply reflectively home afterwards.

I've asked lots of questions of many people over the years, but wish I'd been more inquisitive of Lieutenant-Colonel **George Hamilton Grahame Montagu Cartwright**. "Buns" Cartwright used to sit and watch the Cricketer Cup finals at Burton Court, Chelsea in the 1970s, saying little, often with an almost imperceptible morsel of scrambled egg on his Old Etonian tie, his memories of combat in the uniform of the Coldstream Guards in the Great War firmly locked away. This grand old man, who had scored a century and taken 10 wickets for Eton against Winchester in 1908, lives on picturesquely in my memory gallery.

Earlier still, I had known a man, Captain **Jim Graham**, who came daily into the Sydney shipping office where I worked, and had survived the Battle of Jutland, a Hellish naval engagement in the First World War. Then there was another man who had been in San Francisco when the earthquake struck in 1906. Handshakes with history.

As this introductory chapter neared completion I took the precaution of checking the index of my autobiography *Caught England, Bowled Australia* (1997) just in case I'd overlooked any encounter of significance. I had: several dozen of them.

There was **Harry "Bull" Alexander** at the Melbourne Centenary Test, the chunky, hostile fellow who pounded Jardine in the final Bodyline Test. He later paid the unpopular Pom skipper high tribute for the guts he showed that day. A few years later "Bull" found himself in a much greater conflict – in Crete in one of the fiercest fighting episodes of the Second World War.

Conrad Hunte, a devout Christian who gave West Indies such stability at the top of their batting order in the 1960s, created an amusing whodunnit in 1992 when, as ICC match referee for the ill-tempered England v Pakistan Test at Old Trafford, he refused to explain what he had said in the dressing-rooms after an on-field rumpus. We chased him all over Old Trafford that evening, but even when cornered he refused to elucidate. It all seemed so unnecessary. Why could he not have said simply that he had warned one or both sides about their behaviour? We were left to assume, which is never ideal.

As chance would have it, a couple of days later Hunte, a deeply religious man with happy eyes, guested for a touring team from Georgia (USA) at Godalming, Surrey. I was down to play for the local side. It was a privilege to stand at slip and watch the hero of the 1960-61 Brisbane tied Test match score 60, a run for every year of his age. At close of play would he dash off? Well, he tried to. Only a few minutes after everyone had showered and sought the first beer, Mr Hunte was taking his leave of the company. I had to know what had happened at Old Trafford, so I chased after him (yet again) and confronted him in the dusk outside the old Godalming pavilion. I endeavoured to be casual and diplomatic, and he was predictably polite, but it took some persistence on my part to get him to explain. Eventually he gave his behaviour at the Test some shape: in spite of the intemperate behaviour of some of the Pakistan players, particularly towards umpire Roy Palmer, he had felt it necessary to caution the England players as well because he sensed they were becoming hot under the collar. It was a reasoning that would not have appealed to any Englishman because the fault seemed firmly with one or two over-excited Pakistanis. As ever, though, Conrad Hunte concluded the matter with that gleaming Louis Armstrong smile, and the world continued to rotate.

Jeffrey Barnard, the "professional inebriate", comes into the picture. In a match at Burton Court, Chelsea between teams representing the memory of John Ruskin and Whistler to mark the centenary of their famous court case, we dressed in period costume and had fun. My moustache kept falling off when I batted, so I skipped across to the square leg umpire, Mr Barnard, and handed him my moustache. His confused look caused giggling all over the field. Later, **Mike Hooper**, the charming Surrey player who was to die so young, apologised for slamming four after four off my bowling, a touching and novel gesture. "It's all right," I told this Charterhouse product, "that's what I'm here for."

Mention of Charterhouse sparks recall of one of the most delightful discoveries and interviews I ever undertook. It was with **Wilfrid Timms**, an 83-year-old who had once, as an 18-year-old, scored 154 not out for Northants against Essex. Frail but clear of mind, he looked back with understandable pride at his achievement and also at having captained his county at 18, there having been no other amateur available. In the presence of a man possessed of such a clear memory, it was yet another gripping instance of walking back through time. Mr Timms became a master at Charterhouse, and taught young Peter May cricket and French.

These ramblings, I guess, have to end, though names continue to flood the memory bank: **Joe Goldman**, a survivor of the ghastly combat at Passchendaele and the early king among cricket collectors, with his delight at a bit of price teasing as he disposed of his holdings piece by piece; the eccentric **Tony Baer**, leader in the next generation of collectors, who left us in peals of laughter after proposing first to my daughter and then to my wife; the dignified **Molly Hide**, England's female Hammond, with whom it was a privilege to sit and listen during a women's international at Guildford; **Gary Mason**, British heavyweight champion doomed to die in a road accident, who desperately wanted to learn how to bowl a wrong'un (I tried, believe me) and who finally held the third catch popped up to him by John Morris in the Bunburys match at Wembley, the event watched by Leonard Cheshire; *Cider with Rosie* author and cricket-lover **Laurie Lee**, whose reaction to being asked to write was "The fee isn't much, is it?" (Happily it proved sufficient to tempt him.) What a precious, entertaining cavalcade of people. How lucky I've been.

Should any currently famous cricketer by remote chance happen to read this book, it is to be hoped that it might help him to realise that while his career ought to be enjoyed to the full, retirement (or rejection) must follow. In the years ahead he could even end up wishing for somebody to come along and request an autograph and ask him to recount a few of his memories. By that stage of life he may have come to realise that it is common courtesy to make the signature legible rather than to dispense an insulting squiggle. After all, we're all just leaves being swept down the steady-flowing river of life, some of the leaves larger and more colourful than others.

The sub-title of my autobiography was *A Cricket Slave's Complex Story* (1997), and it seems to have been confirmed that this (the slave bit) was not an inaccurate description. In his generous foreword to *Frith on Cricket*, the anthology published in 2010, John Woodcock wrote that there was a trace of the 18th Century essayist Joseph Addison's "touchy, testy, pleasant fellow" about me. That, I suppose, is something it would be pointless to challenge. It's not comfortable being a perfectionist, especially in this bizarre modern world in which people seem more careless, confused and unreliable than their predecessors. I have little doubt that the fuzzy minds of the drug-taking generation of the 1960s and their successors are at the root of any explanation.

As for Addison, it is not necessarily unpleasant to be compared to that bewigged fellow since his essays were said to have a "breezy, conversational style". But I would wish to distance myself from the criticism of him penned by Bishop Hurd. The bishop objected to Addison's weakness in ending sentences with prepositions, dubbing this flaw an "Addisonian termination", an aberration that, as somebody who cares deeply about our deteriorating language, I believe I've never been guilty of. (Not altogether subtle joke.)

Enough of these handshakes and ramblings. Come and meet some more of my late friends and acquaintances in cricket.

Leslie Ames
1905-1990
"Yours, Les!"

LESLIE AMES kept wicket for England in the five Bodyline Tests of 1932-33. In 47 Test matches altogether between 1929 and 1939 he made 97 dismissals behind the stumps, averaged 40 with the bat and registered eight centuries, including a whirlwind 123 runs before lunch on the third day of the 1935 Oval Test against South Africa. (It was an extended session of play, but it was a remarkable record performance nonetheless, set by a highly popular and respected cricketer.)

For Kent, in a career stretching from 1926 to 1951, he scored nearly 29,000 runs and 78 of his 102 centuries. And he completed over 700 dismissals for the county behind the stumps (239 of them off Tich Freeman's legspin), 972 in all first-class cricket (with an amazing total of 417 stumpings), plus 149 catches in the field. His tally of 128 dismissals in 1929 will never be surpassed.

Ames: a wicketkeeper who, rare for his time, could have played for his batting alone

These are heavyweight statistics. Yet Les radiated absolutely no ego. You respected him instantly. He was calm, dependable, superb: a man who later served cricket in administrative roles. Not least important, my Dad won a few shillings on Les Ames's century against Australia in the Lord's Test match of 1934.

That was Hedley Verity's match: 15 wickets, including Bradman twice, the second time off a steepling top edge. England's victory probably rested upon this cloud-bursting catch being secured. Ames recalled that with the ball the size of a pea in the sky, Wally Hammond at slip murmured: "Yours." Les was not a man to fluster. He held it. England won: their only Lord's victory in an

Ashes Test between 1896 and 2009.

One special day in September 1970, when he was Kent's manager, I got him to sign his autobiography in their dressing-room. Under his signature he wrote: "The day we won the Championship at The Oval." The hop county had last won it in 1913, when Les was seven.

One evening, when he was 80, he was strolling along the Mound Stand concourse at Lord's when the subject of his crippling lumbago came up. All his adult life he had been hampered by attacks How did he feel now? With that he dropped low into the wicketkeeping crouch then rose swiftly and painlessly to his full height. We both laughed.

Phenomenal figures behind the stumps, especially stumpings: here Ames appeals against South Africa's Tuppy Owen-Smith in 1929, Hammond at slip

That year he was honoured at a reception in the House of Commons, taking the adulation in his stride. When his wife Bunty decided she'd had enough of all the kissing by guests as they arrived, she called out in mock alarm: "Les, can't you stop all these people kissing me? There's all this Aids about, and you never know!" Her husband just smiled. Ex-RAF, he was the cool and calm type, even when an England tour of Pakistan was disrupted by civil unrest. As manager he delayed the decision to abandon the tour until there was no sensible alternative. Most of the players had already long since decided they'd had enough.

He was also a shrewd analyst, and became the first professional to be appointed as a Test selector. He had insight, and to hear him comparing Verity and Underwood was to be part of a masterclass. And imagine the fascination of seeing him watching for the first time film of himself keeping wicket to Harold Larwood in the Bodyline Tests. Having seen the programme beforehand, I urged him and a few others to watch it when it was shown during the 1977 Centenary Test in Melbourne. We dumped ourselves on chairs and beds in that crowded room, and just as the key clip of Larwood came on, I nudged him: "Watch this!"

Although during his playing days there had never been any serious murmur that Larwood threw the ball, this sequence, shot from long-off during the 1933 Brisbane Test, seemed a touch incriminating (as it does for many a bowler from that position). I watched Les Ames from side-on. "Well, I never!" he gasped, wide-eyed. The leg-side bouncer ended up in the young Ames's upstretched gloves close to leg slip. The older Ames was quite stunned. Was the camera deceiving us? Probably, he thought.

Like Wally Hammond, he had disliked Bodyline; but as a professional he knew he had to keep his opinion to himself. It was a matter of loyalty. The crisis passed, as all things pass. Les Ames died in 1990. Like most of that generation, he is greatly missed.

John Arlott
1914-1991
Most Famous Voice in England

I HEARD his distinctive Hampshire tones on the wireless when the South Africans were in England in 1947. That boy had no way of knowing that in years to come John Arlott would become his closest friend in cricket, a surrogate father. Some of us need a helping hand, and it was John who eased my way into the world of cricket-writing by urging E.W.Swanton in 1972 to take me on as deputy editor of *The Cricketer*.

Why did John do this? I can only suppose that, having gauged my commitment to cricket, something clicked, despite our mild political differences and disparate backgrounds – not so disparate in origin perhaps in that neither of us had known any vestige of benefit from privilege.

First the sighting in Sydney in 1955, a florid-faced JA in white shirt, hating the heat and humidity and irritably telling another lad: "No, son, I'm not

The author with John Arlott at the master broadcaster's welcoming home in Hampshire, mid-1960s

Denis Compton!" Then, in 1966, the first approach, to have a book signed in the Lord's press-box, to chat briefly; later a letter, and by return an invitation to call in at his large, cosy home in Alresford, with its overwhelming library and wine cellar. He recognised my hopes and sensed my devotion to the game and its history, and the friendship deepened, compatibility established.

For the next quarter-century we mused and argued and laughed and helped each other and dined and drank, mostly around his incomparable oak table, where the company was always good and time didn't matter. The amount of wine sunk was prodigious, the conversation vibrant, uninhibited, laughter ever-present. Dishes as exotic as lampries might be served.

We did the rounds of antique markets, and I often drove him during Test matches, disappointed whenever he fell asleep on the return journey. Failing health and love of home eventually curtailed his life on the road.

As the most famous voice in England during those halcyon years he alone was excused from announcing himself when telephoning. The thespian in him incorporated an expressive grunt when in doubt or prone to debate. We fell out only once, a silly spat on the principle of expenses. He looked sad as I departed, and telephoned next morning, greatly to my relief.

John became a bastion of the new magazine *Wisden Cricket Monthly* from the

A discussion during the making of the Golden Great Batsmen video programme, 1982

tense and exciting time of its launch in 1979 until we lost him. He preferred to write about his early Hampshire heroes, compelling me to search carefully for when he'd last written about, say, Lionel Tennyson. And when, on visits, I was asked to sample the latest white wine, my reaction sometimes disappointed him and sent him to the cellar for some appealing red, impeccable host that he was.

The shadow in his soul was displayed through the black tie he wore from the time of his young son's death on the road in 1965. I was not alone in believing that he spent the rest of his life seeking some sort of refuge in his glorious broadcasting and writing career and in the company of friends, with the indispensable clink of glasses. And I detected early that he could not bear to be alone.

From his 200 short but expressive letters, one sentence [in 1970] says much: "I shall be up at Lord's with no assistance and, if you would like to share the commentary box and a bottle of claret with me, you could then have the responsibility of taking over the broadcast if I faint."

His exile on Alderney after 1980 didn't help. He was now much more than a half-hour drive away. I was his last visitor from the mainland. He now had a respirator strapped to his mouth. The gathering chattered away while he just sat there. Then he looked across and winked, a gesture I saw as meaning "I've been chattering away all my life. Now it's my turn to sit here and listen to you lot!"

I drove him down to the sea-lashed rocks and we sipped brandy from absurd smuggled polystyrene cups. "I shan't live much longer," he whispered. I tried to find the words, but we both knew that he knew what he was talking about – as ever.

Trevor Bailey
1923-2011
Always the Forward Defensive

ONE DAY in the Sydney summer of 1950-51, I was browsing in Bert Oldfield's shop when in walked two members of the MCC (England) touring team, Trevor Bailey and Reg Simpson. There was some idle chatter and they signed my autograph book. In later years I came to know both well. A ball from Lindwall had broken Bailey's right thumb, which was now throbbing beneath plaster. The tortured signature was thus all but a mystery. Who was this "Trov Baxter"?

"Barnacle" or "Barndoor" Bailey: the most famous – or infamous – defensive batsman of his time

He was excused, naturally. In fact the signature seemed rather special. But the hidden joke was that years later I discovered that Trevor Bailey's *normal* signature was *always* a coil of scribble.

He was a study: obstinate, tough as teak, even irritating, as his opponents well knew. He was also unpredictable. Bump into him and wife Greta on the east coast of Barbados and he'd be light-hearted and affable; by the Warner

Stand at lunch during a Test, as we drank David Lemmon's claret, he'd be withdrawn; walking across the Edgbaston car park, he'd suddenly speak of witnessing the horrors of Belsen as a young Royal Marine in 1945; musing at the MCG, I once recalled a flying gully catch he'd taken down on that very field. He waved the reverie aside: "Long, long ago!"

At Sydney in 1954 he strode to the middle, chest thrust out as if on the parade ground, slender captain Len Hutton by his side. I was so proud of them. The heart pounded (mine, and maybe his and Len's too) as England weathered a haunting opening burst from Lindwall and Archer on a dampish pitch. After 20 minutes, Trevor (0) lost his middle stump to Lindwall. Two months later, at the same handsome venue, he presented his wicket – a touch ostentatiously – to a struggling Lindwall because, with the match drifting to a draw, having made 72, he thought the great and widely admired Aussie's Test days were about to end with a tantalising 99 England wickets.

It was a wicked script: at Melbourne four years later Lindwall was still around to inflict a "pair" on him in what became Bailey's final Test match. That 1958-59 series had begun with his outrageous 68 at Brisbane in 7½ hours. On the half-hour train ride home from work my bulky portable radio told of

Trevor Bailey's characteristic nonchalance is evident in this previously unpublished picture taken by the author in the Sydney Test of 1958-59

Even Bailey's smile, captured here by John Woodcock, seemed to hint that he retained a little secret

three maybe four singles all the way from St James to Hurstville.

Lo! – a third of a century on, I found myself "batting" alongside Trevor Bailey on a television programme called *Devil's Advocate*. It was something of a set-up. On "hot seats" illuminated by lurid red lamps and before a studio audience divisively placed on two banks of seating, one for Pakistani and West Indian cricket enthusiasts (Clive Lloyd and the excitable Haseeb Ahsan among them), another for Caucasians (Fred Trueman in the front row), Trevor and I were grilled by "advocate" Darcus Howe, a London-based West Indian. It was supposed that Trevor and I were consumed with resentment and suspicion over everything non-English. Did we think that the Pakistan pace bowlers tampered with the ball? Did we believe that the West Indies fast bowlers were unduly hostile?

A tape of the programme shows that Trevor, voice more taut than usual, was uncomfortable. He tried to pursue a jocular placatory line, whereas I was irate, telling our interrogator that his suggestion that our published remarks on brutal bowling and ball-tampering were racially motivated was pitiful. It was as if Trevor was playing that renowned forward defensive or swaying out of the way of a fusillade of bouncers from Heine and Adcock all over again. I was wishing he would play a hook or two. Remember that out-of-character six he hit at Brisbane to earn £100?

The barracking to our right was momentarily silenced when Trueman, on the facing bank, finally got into gear on the subject of Pakistan's umpires. The programme ended in near-chaos, though the final edit smoothed the edges. I can't say for certain whether the Bailey-Frith partnership quite forced a draw. Hot topics like these seldom result in amendments to viewpoints.

The next time Trevor and I bumped into each other we were glad simply to sit and sip.

David Bairstow

1951-1998

Exuberance and Sensitivity

IT REALLY stirred things up when burly wicketkeeper David "Bluey" Bairstow was summoned to join the England team in Australia in January 1979 after deputy 'keeper Roger Tolchard's cheekbone had been shattered. There we were, in peaceful Tasmania, when "Bairs" arrived like a whirlwind and took the field as a substitute. He was jet-lagged, red-faced and vocal, and his first touch of the ball, at short third man, resulted hilariously in a throw that nearly decapitated the umpire at square leg.

During lunch Bairstow had a lot to say for himself, a welcome distraction from the frozen relations between two other Yorkshiremen in the room, Geoff Boycott and John Hampshire, who were trying to ignore each other. But that's another story. On the second day Bluey was late for lunch, having toppled onto a concrete floor while doing stretching exercises. There he sat, florid of face, nose redder still and throbbing after the fall, white bloodstained towel around his chunky shoulders. When a buxom waitress piled his plate high he joked that he must be suffering from double vision. His eyes continued to flash from one person to another in that crowded room.

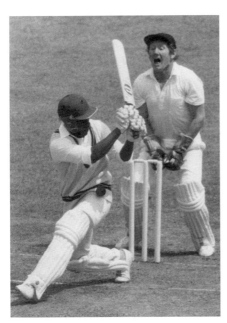

Raucous "Bluey" Bairstow in his domain behind the stumps

By the time the team and media party reached Adelaide, Bairstow had calmed down somewhat, though on the rest day of the Test match he was uncontrollable in Wyndie Hill Smith's swimming pool during the great Barossa Valley winemaker's memorable open day. Bluey plunged in time and again, like a deranged dolphin. Scyld Berry threw volleys of lemons from the far end. Bairstow flung himself into the water to catch them at full stretch from one side of the pool, while I did likewise from the other. It vaguely occurred to me that if our heads were to clash – which seemed a certainty – our skulls would surely be fractured (well, mine anyway). That would be all right for him: England would simply enlist a fourth tour wicketkeeper. However, as a freelance writer, I would have been in considerable trouble. But we'd all had far too much Yalumba red and/or white to worry. And, my goodness, David Bairstow not only knew how to have fun: he was also a ferocious competitor.

On the return flight to England, as we descended to Heathrow, assistant manager Ken Barrington ordered the players to smarten up. Bluey returned from the toilet cubicle having accidentally nicked his throat. This takes some doing with an electric razor. I had also thought it interesting when he

Bairstow with Ray Illingworth and the author at the 1979 launching of Wisden Cricket Monthly

signed my tour book with a slightly grandiloquent "David L.Bairstow" while everyone else simply wrote their names without middle initials.

Months later he was back in Australia and smashing a memorable 21 not out under the SCG lights as he and Graham Stevenson stole a thrilling one-dayer from a stupefied Lillee and Thomson. England, near death at 129 for 8, had still needed a further 35 runs in six overs. "Loov'leh neight for it, in't'it?" chuckled Stevenson as he passed the bemused Aussies. Yorkshiremen everywhere were filled with pride that night on an otherwise gloomy tour.

In between those two tours of Australia, David Bairstow was one of the Yorkshire players who came along to the launch of *Wisden Cricket Monthly* in 1979, when the Northerners were playing at Lord's. That merry night was rendered all the happier by the regular gusts of Bairstow laughter.

His career ended before he wanted it to, and he was soon floundering. In the sponsors' tent one evening he was flogging World Cup ties and talking even more loudly than usual. Yet in the Taverners' "Ashes" match at Wormsley in 1992 he seemed subdued. He'd wanted his career to go on – perhaps forever. And this exuberant cricketer was a great deal more sensitive than outsiders realised. No longer being centrestage disturbed him. He'd been out there in the middle since he was only sixteen. Financial, marital and health problems followed, compounded by a drink-drive charge. And before we knew it he was gone, suicide by rope, surely cricket's greatest shock of the 1990s. You have to hand it to the Yorkies. Pallbearer Phil Carrick, a team-mate for years, quipped: "Ah've carried t'booger out of a few places in m'time, but never in."

Those who remember the explosive "Bluey" Bairstow are now drawing an especially deep pleasure from the success of his son Jonny.

Fred Bakewell
1908-1983
Fit to Bat with Bradman

"HE'S SOMETHING of a wandering minstrel and a sad case," said the Northamptonshire secretary in 1976 when I asked how I might find Fred Bakewell. He was correct on the first count. It took several years of enquiry before the ill-fated old Northants and England batsman was found. Alfred Harry Bakewell could not understand why somebody would want to place a microphone in front of him after all this time. Yet his tragically brief career had been spectacular and I wanted to know more.

Fred Bakewell missed at backward square by Jack Hearne in Northamptonshire's match against Middlesex at Lord's in 1932. The wicketkeeper is Fred Price

"I don't think I missed a match for the county from 1928 to 1936, apart from Test appearances [there were six]," he said softly. Through defeat after defeat he was the spinal column of the county's batting, hammering runs and curtailing the embarrassment of his struggling club. Of their 250 matches in the 1930s, Northants, poor devils, won only 18. From a crab-like stance ("Who worries too much so long as you're hitting the ball?") Bakewell, sharp of reflex, launched into the bowling, once taking five fours off Frank Smailes' opening over in a Championship match at Harrogate.

Four of his 31 centuries were above 200, the last of these an unbeaten 241 at Chesterfield, poignantly only hours before the car crash that ended it all. His skipper, Reggie Northway, who was at the wheel of the open-top sports-car, was killed. Fred's skull and right arm were fractured and the flesh was torn from his hands. He was in hospital for weeks, then tried so hard to overcome the painful physical legacy. Eventually he had to declare "I'm finished". His career as a top cricketer was over and he was only twenty-seven.

With his wife Dorothy and DF, St Albans, 1981

The complete absence of regret or bitterness moved me: "Just one of those things that happened," he said with a shrug. "You have to just accept it." He had been seen as the natural successor as an England opener to Herbert Sutcliffe (for whom he sacrificed his wicket in a run-out mix-up in the 1931 Oval Test). That is how good he was. And Bakewell, wearing no protection at all, was as wonderful a short-leg fieldsman as he was a fearless stroke-player.

It was his personality that fascinated. In the shadows of his life story lurked rumours of sleeping rough, snubbing authority, shoplifting charges, a nature that embraced, in Robertson-Glasgow's view, "a dull thread of negligence, even apathy", leaving him "in need of a leader-manager", though Fred would not have been comfortable with the army of supernumeraries in today's England dressing-room. He was, after all, a man who "could have batted with Bradman on not uneven terms". There was "authority" about his batting.

His Test century came in 1933 against West Indies at The Oval (the surviving film clips convey a sense of defiance and confidence as he steered England from crisis towards innings victory). He made 85 in his next Test that winter at Madras, then 63 and 54 in the 1935 Manchester Test against South

Africa, showing that he belonged at the highest level. That Oval hundred? "Just like reaching a century in a county match . . . or even a village match."

While he might have fumbled to recall what he had done the previous day, his memory for cricket past was clear. He and young Alex Snowden were sozzled from birthday champagne when they went out and smashed 199 opening the batting against Kent at Dover. This opening pair also posted a century for the first wicket *twice in one day* at Edgbaston. Bakewell even hooked Larwood for six at Kettering. "That's a short ground," he murmured. But against that bruising Notts attack at Trent Bridge in 1935 he hit 143, winning some money from the Chief Constable of Nottingham in doing so.

As soon as he knew that his time at the top was over he gave away all his cricket gear. He became a village publican, but more grief followed, including another car accident that cost him an eye in 1965. The parallels with another popular Northants and England batsman, Colin Milburn, were chilling. I shed a quiet tear for Fred Bakewell whenever I catch sight of the MCC tie he was given as an honorary member, passed on to me by his widow.

The attempt to pad up again and renew his broken career
proved futile for Bakewell

S.F.Barnes

1873-1967

The Greatest Bowler?

"WHAT DO you want?" A nice greeting, I must say, to a pilgrim who had just driven for three hours all the way up to Cannock, Staffordshire. It was not as if my visit was unscheduled. Sydney Barnes had agreed to it by telephone. He was now 94, and still ferociously sharp mentally. And here I was, looking up into that gaunt face framed in the doorway, and wondering if I was ever going to be ushered inside.

Maybe he was playing games, teasing, provoking? The history books tell us how difficult he could be to captains, committees and opponents. Now he even refused to sign a book because I had only a ballpoint pen. His copperplate handwriting with a fountain pen – or was it a quill? – was renowned. "I'm not going into the office for you just to get my pen," he croaked. It was a Saturday, so the Council office in Stafford where he worked part-time would be locked up anyway.

He took some warming up. Then the stories began to flow, though I can't recall a real smile throughout that awesome session in the living-room – a faintly evil grimace, yes. Animatedly he talked me through his first-morning spell against Australia at Melbourne in the 1911-12 Ashes series: bowled Bardsley with his first ball, had Kelleway lbw, bowled Hill, then had Armstrong caught by his Warwickshire wicketkeeper "Tiger" Smith: 4 for 1 in seven legendary overs.

Having Minnett later caught by Hobbs gave Barnes 5 for 6, all quality wickets, and England were on their way to sweeping the series after the first Test had been lost. That'd show his vain England captain J.W.H.T.Douglas that Barnes and

Even in his nineties S.F.Barnes exuded a faintly intimidatory air

55

not he should share the new ball with Frank Foster.

Barnes revealed that the man who brought a bottle of whisky to him in his room the night before, after word had circulated that he was sick, was none other than the Australian veteran, little Syd Gregory, who was not playing in this Test match. It made a world of difference next day. "SF" was as fiery as ever, shocking Australia with that 11-over spell, later flopping to the turf when he was barracked for slow field arrangement, resuming only when the noise stopped.

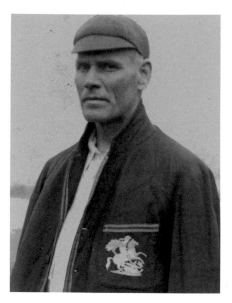

In England uniform, the gaze militant and forbidding

Did he cut the ball like Derek Underwood? *"Cut* it!" He glared at me, and again I wondered if he was about to hurl something my way. "I *spun* the ball!" Those long, gnarled fingers gyrated around imaginary leather. He bowled a brisk medium, but applied spin, with excruciating accuracy. No wonder he was regarded as the greatest bowler of all by most thoughtful judges. His bag of 49 wickets in South Africa in 1913-14 is *still* a Test series record. And he missed the fifth Test! The official reasons were hazy, but Barnes now explained: they wouldn't pay for his wife's accommodation.

He was then forty, and that marked the end of his erratic Test career: 189 wickets at 16.43 in 27 Tests. Had he played as many Tests as Shane Warne (as yet unborn when we met) S.F.Barnes might have finished with around a thousand wickets, although covered pitches would have cut him back a little (my view, not his).

Like most old-timers, he had a distant look in his eyes as he recalled long-ago incidents and events: England's one-wicket victory which he pulled off with Arthur Fielder at Melbourne in 1908, and his feigned injury when the fee offered for playing in the Lord's Centenary match in 1914 was reckoned inadequate. There didn't seem to be a sentimental bone in his body. Money drove him beyond most other considerations. He went from league club to league club because the pay in county cricket fell short. He had as little respect for committees as for opposing batsmen. This theme saturated his reminiscing.

Years later the great South African offspinner Hugh Tayfield passed on to me some extreme advice that S.F.Barnes had given him: "Don't take any notice of anything anybody ever tells you!"

It was slightly demanding as well as pleasurable to be in Syd Barnes's company. He was a nonagenarian, yet his brooding countenance gave a vivid taste of what it must have been like to be an opposing batsman.

He wasn't all malevolence, real or synthetic. As I was leaving he relented and signed my book.

Not an express bowler, but Syd Barnes oozed ferocity

Charles Barnett
1910-1993
Close to the Elite

HOW WOULD you feel if, having creamed your way to 98, you have one over remaining before lunch on the opening day of an Ashes Test match but you have lost the strike? Bill O'Reilly is about to bowl and your partner, young Ashes debutant Len Hutton, has 61 by his name. Would you urge him to seek a quick single? Not Charles Barnett. The unselfish 28-year-old senior man came striding down the pitch to tell the young Yorkshireman to play safely for lunch, which he did, blocking out a maiden over. They came in at the interval at Trent Bridge on that June day in 1938 with 169 for 0 on the board, the launch-pad for England's ultimate 658 for 8 in a drawn four-day match in which seven centuries and many records were registered – and yet it is commonly referred to as "McCabe's match" after the dashing Australian's 232.

I often sat with Barnett during the 1970s as he solemnly carried out his task as match adjudicator at county one-dayers. As the sun crossed the sky we chatted away; or rather, I listened. From a county debut at 16 in 1927, son and nephew of earlier Gloucestershire batsmen, he became a proud and dignified man, an amateur who turned professional, with a vaguely aristocratic manner about him. And he used to bat with all the thrilling freedom of the amateur, excelling in the booming drive.

Like Wally Hammond, with whom he shared so many spectacular stands, he also bowled briskly and was outstanding in the field. So his was one of the more meaningful opinions about the mighty but moody Hammond. Charles was guarded, unwilling to damage the sense of loyalty that was endemic to men of his generation, so he extolled Hammond's great cricket abilities with enthusiasm, largely leaving what was unsaid as a means of explaining how difficult it could be to share a dressing-room with him.

Barnett's record abounded with exciting stroke-laden innings, the highest 259 against Queensland in 1936-37, on his only Australian tour. He kept a letter Douglas Jardine had sent him: the former Test skipper urged him to vary his method against Australia's little demon spinner Clarrie Grimmett, to play him naturally "like Wally" but to avoid going forward to every ball: "Grimmett likes it to be all forward or all back – even I used to play forward sometimes just to upset him! I think you have as good a chance of giving

Charles Barnett sweeps O'Reilly during the 1936-37 Ashes series

Grimmett and O'Reilly stick as anyone."

In the event, Grimmett was to be dumped by Australia's selectors. Barnett made 129 in almost six hours at Adelaide in a losing cause (and ran out the debutant Ross Gregory for 51 with a direct throw). England famously conceded the series after being two up.

His generation were cheated of six years of cricket by the war (in the 1936-37 team photo he stands between Hedley Verity and Ken Farnes, both to be killed in action), but he did play on afterwards, when past his best. His rosy cheeks flushed when someone in our group referred to Charlie's shop in Cheltenham as a "butcher's shop", for it was actually a slightly up-market establishment where he sold fish and game. Always a countryman at heart, he was still riding with the Berkeley Hunt when of pensionable age, and enthused in a letter that he felt the same thrill on horseback as before a big match: "When you ride at a big black hedge and know there is a bloody great ditch that will take a horse and rider out of sight it is frightening but I love it."

Like most old cricketers, he was critical of some later batsmen's techniques but blamed naïve coaches rather than the youngsters themselves. He devoted some of his own time to coaching and once proudly had six of his lads captaining public school teams. If only they could fully have appreciated just how exciting a batsman C.J.Barnett himself had been.

As a matter of interest, on that great day at Trent Bridge in 1938 Barnett and Hutton posted 219, the first stand of 200 for England for any wicket in a home Ashes Test match. Barnett reached his century off the first ball after lunch, from the legspinner Frank Ward. That is how close he came to joining Trumper, Macartney and Bradman on a truly elite honour roll.

*A professional with the air of an
adventurous amateur*

Ken Barrington
1930-1981
"No rushing," he cautioned

SITTING BY the picket fence, I too felt the strain. Ken Barrington was closing in on his second hundred of the Sydney Test match, but Davidson, McKenzie and Hawke had reduced him to strokeless stalemate. Australian wicketkeeper Wally Grout summed Barrington up by saying that you could almost see the Union Jack floating behind him, but this day he was utterly becalmed as the twin-hundreds honour dangled tantalisingly before him and the field seemed impenetrable.

He had made England safe as this turgid 1962-63 series drew to a close (1-1), as he had so often done, but was then caught by Grout off McKenzie six short of what would have been his third century on the trot. Trot? Nowadays, whenever I watch Jonathan Trott at his unshiftable best, I can't help but remember Kenny. He was once even dropped by England for slow scoring, a fate unlikely to befall I.J.L.Trott (who, as it happens, was born 39 days after Barrington's shock death in Barbados).

It was my delight to share a cricket field with K.F.Barrington. Back in 1965 we both made ducks in a Micky Stewart benefit match at East Molesey. Ken was so upset at falling to a grubber that he packed his bag and drove home.

Thirteen years later we played for the English Press XI in Sydney. It was a sensational start: Whiting, Martin-Jenkins and Blofeld all gone for ducks, and I'd had my nose tickled by a bouncer off the dodgy surface. I

England had no more dedicated batsman in the 1960s

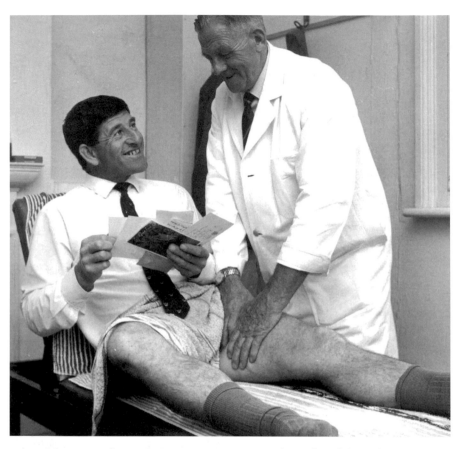

Like most professionals, Ken Barrington was not always free of physical niggles

perceived then what a comfort it must always have been for Ken's partners to have his chunky, reassuring shape at the other end.

Suppressing the unnerving reality of batting with a man whose record embodied not only an average of 64 against Australia, 20 Test centuries, and also one heart attack, I thumped a ball into the long field and tore off for a two or three – only to find him walking a single. "No rushing," he cautioned. "I don't want another heart attack." Those pale, craggy features showed that he meant what he said. We hung on for some while, and England's dignity once again was restored.

He was also supportive on the golf course. In a Lord's Taverners event, he'd been quietly observing my efforts through four or five holes. "Try slowing down the backswing," he muttered. That was all. Good advice. This was the yeoman who became the beloved father figure to Gooch's England XI.

Then there was the time when, astonishingly, I saw Ken and John Arlott having a go at each other in the old Oval press-box one evening. Unlikely though it seemed, it was something to do with their respective earnings. Both men were proud of their modest backgrounds and of their achievements. Around that time another unusual occurrence was observed. Ken, having batted defiantly for hours for his country, and now showered and changed, spotted an exasperated Arlott scratching his head in the Oval forecourt because his car, bonnet raised, wouldn't start. Ken was a qualified mechanic. He strolled over, rolled up his sleeves, spent some time tinkering with the Arlott limo, and got him started. It was a memorable interlude.

Ken Barrington was famous for his malapropisms. Among the most cherished were: "That was good bowling in anybody's cup of tea"; and (to a bowler): "You've got him in two man's land!" On the rare occasions when he got a good night's sleep he would say that he "slept like a lark".

His innate kindness showed in many ways. Shaming the illegible graffiti usually scribbled by modern Test cricketers, he would place a well-written "To David with all my very Best Wishes Ken Barrington" on the fly-leaf. In 1975 he even travelled, with Geoff Arnold, to a store to help promote my book *The Fast Men*. There was no fee involved, just a nice lunch.

His death on the second night of the Barbados Test in March 1981 was as stunning and shattering a loss as English cricket has ever sustained. Next morning I saw cricketers weeping.

It may easily be understood, perhaps, that I am reluctant to update my old car: the number plate includes the initials KFB. Surely sentimentality is no crime?

Ever ready to do a favour, even endorsing David Frith's 1975 book

Sir Alec Bedser
1918-2010
Lion of a Man

ALEC BEDSER sent down the first ball I witnessed in a Test match. He was also the first Test cricketer with whom I had a chat. Sydney, January 1951: that lion of a man had carried the attack, as usual, with England two bowlers short after injury. I can still readily picture that stout performance, and can hear the smack of the ball pulled lustily by Loxton into Alec's huge hands. A day or so later, with near-identical twin Eric, he had talked for some time to this lad outside the team hotel, unknowingly pointing me in a fateful direction. Ambitions to be a barrister or architect were scrapped. I now knew that I needed to be a cricket writer: nothing more nor less.

Over the decades I came to know Alec so well that we could argue freely without repercussions. And boy, could he be grumpy. In 1958 I raced out to the SCG on my motor-scooter to find that MCC had crushed NSW: what had happened; who'd done the damage? Now a tour manager, he was standing with captain Peter May. His curt retort: "We won, didn't we!" All I'd wanted

The steady Bedser bowling action, seldom if ever subject to breakdown

to know was who had taken the wickets, and how. Never mind.

Just over 10 years later, at The Oval, scene of his many triumphs for Surrey, a tour of Australia was looming. At the press conference I ventured to ask if he approved of extended series (this one was to consist of _seven_ Tests). He replied that he didn't – "But don't quote me!"

Once, when he was doing his press-box rounds, we asked for the reasoning behind Underwood's replacement by Gifford. The latter, he explained with characteristic certainty, flighted the ball more. Problem was that at that moment "Giff" was whacking ball after ball in on a yorker length. As for any sense of grace, when we surrounded him after Botham had stepped down from the captaincy after his pair at Lord's in '81, dear old Alec simply growled: "We were about to sack him anyway."

In 1973 I was sent to Scarborough at considerable cost to serve as one of the match judges. Bev Congdon did enough with bat and ball, but when I found Alec in the pavilion melee to give him my vote, he brushed me and it aside, saying that Lance Cairns (who smacked a few late sixes) was the choice. The third judge later told me he hadn't been consulted either. Alec was simply physically too large to challenge.

Nor was sitting next to him at dinners always such a rewarding experience. Only a five-star speaker could earn his approval. Under his breath he would moan about the quality and the length of the address, whether it be Benny Green on his hero Compton or Stan Sismey on the Australian Services tour of 1945.

Then there was the time Alec handed out the pewter mugs to those of us who had taken part in the Bunburys D-Day commemorative match at The Oval. As he thrust the trinket into my sweaty palm he couldn't resist a belated chastisement: "You played across that ball!" I tried to excuse myself by suggesting that he had probably never once in his illustrious career had to contend with _ten_ fielders spread across the cover

The Surrey and England lion

65

field. He simply grunted.

There were plenty of good times, usually when we shared a moan or two about the state of the game, lousy bowling, indiscreet strokeplay. This Trojan who led England's bowling for seven years was ferociously proud of having dismissed Don Bradman six times in Tests, and would describe each triumph in sharp detail. Yet life mostly seemed grim. Perhaps he should have married.

Only two years ago I think I found the real Alec Bedser. He agreed to an interview for the Imperial War Museum's sound archive. The brothers served in the RAF military and, lucky to survive a close machine-gun spray on a French beach, they ended up in Italy, guarding British assets against local thieves and saboteurs. It would have needed a lot of Italian courage to have taken on those big lads from Surrey.

Above all, the complete absence of phoniness made him so likable. How I miss him, moans and all.

Alec Bedser, with Jim Laker, both also generous enough to endorse a Frith publication

Bill Bowes

1908-1987

Kindly, Resonant, Yorkshire Voice

MOUNTAINOUS FRAME crowned by a balding and bespectacled head of an academic, W.E."Bill" Bowes (as he preferred to sign himself) was a man we always looked forward to seeing in the press-box, an arrival marked by cordial greetings all round in a deep, gentle and resonant voice.

When in tandem with Harold Larwood he looked cumbersome and slightly awkward, but there was great energy in his shuffling delivery after right boot had clicked behind the left. Batsmen hated the sharp bounce he generated with such apparent ease. He bowled the "heavy ball" long before the term was devised.

He was most famous for having bowled Don Bradman with the first ball the Australian faced in the Bodyline series and then getting him out three times in succession in the 1934 Tests (though on these occasions the little champ had made 304, 244 and 77) and again in 1938 (103 this time). It was a nice record but there was never any wild talk of a hoodoo.

In 1943, while in captivity curing the war, Big Bill was given the heartbreaking news of the death of his friend Hedley Verity in the Sicily campaign. Justifiably he was left with a possessive line on his lost team-mate: "What have you been writing about my old pal Hedley then?"

Bowes was a kindly man, and thoughtful. As one-day cricket took hold he advanced an argument that if a batsman's innings is not limited then why should a bowler's spell be? If a bowler was doing well why should he have to stop after a certain number of overs?

As for that 1932-33 tour, he worshipped the England captain, Douglas Jardine. I have the copy of his autobiography which he inscribed to him: "To my friend and greatest of

Bill Bowes takes the field with his bosom pal Hedley Verity

captains – DRJ. May you recapture a few of your triumphs in these pages. 'Bill' Bowes."

The relationship was not always so cordial. Bill enjoyed telling of their stroll through the gardens in Adelaide after he had stubbornly bowled short and been repeatedly pulled to an unguarded boundary in the tourists' match against South Australia. Here was a clash of strong wills. Jardine had refused his repeated requests to have a fieldsman out there. At the end of his tether, Bill pleaded for an extra leg-side fielder. His captain looked down his fine long nose and said in that clipped manner: "No, but you can have three."

They discussed it calmly that evening as they walked among the eucalypts. Jardine made it clear that if Bill challenged his orders he would be on the next ship home. Bill got the point.

A famous Ashes moment: Bradman plays on to Bowes first ball, Melbourne, December 1932

I once took him and John Arlott to a private supper in Leeds during a Test match. Their subtle obligation was to entertain with reminiscence. It was rich material, none more entertaining than Bill's slow description of that Bradman first-ball duck at the MCG. Australia's greatest had missed the first Test, so this was his first innings of the series, though he had endured some red-hot encounters against the Englishmen in preliminary matches. A packed house gave him an extended and tumultuous reception. Play was held up. Bowes's first attempt to bowl had to be aborted. He stood there waiting. To pass the time he signalled long leg to move a few yards. Then, at last, he was free to bowl.

He dug the ball in, Bradman essayed a hook, under-edged, and his stumps resembled a canefield after a cyclone. The stunned MCG crowd were silent. The trams outside could be heard clearly. And the customarily stony-faced Jardine, hands above head, was doing a war dance that to everybody's enormous regret was not filmed.

Cricket-writer Bowes, in the press-box with E.M. Wellings and Bruce Harris

Forty-four years later Bill stood in the enclosure with over 200 other former Ashes cricketers at the Centenary Test at that same MCG as Harold Larwood and Bill Voce were escorted to the middle of the ground. There the two old Bodyliners from Notts removed their coats as if about to bowl. The crowd loved it. Then it struck me that it had been Bill who had got Bradman out that day.

"You should be out there too," I whispered.

"Noa, noa," came the modest response. But there was a distant look in his eyes.

Sir Donald Bradman
1908-2001
Jousting with The Greatest

"SO, DAVID," said Don Bradman, leaning rather menacingly across the lunch table, "you think you know better than me and Dennis Lillee and Richie Benaud and the Chappell brothers?"

Yet again we were debating the front-foot no-ball law, which Don hated. I believed – and still do – that a reversion to the old back-foot law would be retrograde. Bradman was exasperated. His face had reddened. I suppose mine had too. Then his delightful wife Jessie, for surely the umpteenth time in their lives together, eased an awkward situation. "David," she said sweetly, "have you written Don's obituary yet?" No, I hadn't. I wasn't that well organised. And anyway, he was going to live to 100, wasn't he? We all laughed.

The lively disagreements we sometimes had through thirty years of friendship were probably a source of sustenance for Don, who never endured self-doubt. And, like most great men, he inevitably found himself spending much time with fawning yes-men. Yet in one sense he was forever essentially a boy from the bush, gifted with an extraordinary mind and reflexes, fired by ambition and fierce determination: the key to his insistence on always

London 1974: Sir Len Hutton, Sir Don, and DF

being right. The keen-eyed young man with kookaburra features was still discernible in that ageing face.

He once took me to task for writing that he bowled Wally Hammond out with a full-toss at Adelaide in 1933. "It was *not* a full-toss!" But five or six participants in that Test match, including Hammond himself, had declared it

Don Bradman in light-hearted mood on board ship in 1938

to be a full-toss. And I discovered – too late – that Don himself had spoken of it as such in his radio summary very soon after the incident. Amazingly, all these years later, he seemed to regard the bowling of a full-toss as a symptom of defective character. I loved him for that.

His particular turn of humour was displayed in a quiet Adelaide restaurant when the waitress asked him if he'd now like some apple pie. "What makes you think I'd want apple pie?" he teased. "You just look like a man who likes apple pie," she said. With that he said, "Well then I'll have some apple pie!" He began to giggle, and it was contagious. Soon that corner of the restaurant resounded to laughter. Ridiculous but wonderful.

Somewhere in the 120-odd letters I received from him is his reaction to my costly acquisition at auction of Victor Trumper's fob-watch. He kidded that he was now going to hunt through his cupboards: "I reckon I could dig up a couple of wrist-watches."

Since 1930, still cricket's batting king after all these years

He was very generous, contributing forewords to two of my books with scant concern for remuneration, and passing to me all kinds of things he no longer needed, such as early New South Wales yearbooks with his personal rubber stamp on them. Maybe the one thing we truly shared, the red-and-white cap of the St George club, counted for something.

Bradman, who revered cricket's traditions, was a man of adamant opinions. He was laughingly dismissive of a purported history on video, declaring that compiler Ian Chappell's knowledge of cricket history "would fit on a postage stamp". He was content only when he had had the last word in a debate. I suppose it was some sort of substitute for twenty competitive years of habitually carving up bowlers of all descriptions.

Tireless correspondent though he was, he became impatient with birthday cards. "I know I'm 84," he wrote in August 1992. "I don't need reminding. It means I'm one step nearer to the grave." Speaking of which, after one long session at his Adelaide home, he kindly offered to drive me back to the hotel. Just after midnight, as he was steering the car out of Holden Street, a vehicle came speeding towards us out of the blackness to our right. Don Bradman seemed not to have noticed it. White-knuckled, I instinctively cried out. He rammed his foot onto the brake pedal, and we were saved. Calm as ever (apparently), he continued driving, saying not a word about our lucky survival.

I've often reflected on what a glorious way to go that would have been.

Bill Brown
1912-2008
Natural Grace and Elegance

CONVERSATION WITH W.A."Bill" Brown could easily have left the impression that he was just a club cricketer. Although he scored a century at Lord's in 1934 in only his second Test match and carried his bat for 206 at the same ground four years later, memories of these and the Trent Bridge hundred and numerous other big scores for Australia and Queensland were simply not for discussion. He was infuriatingly reticent.

It went further than that. During a chat one sleepy afternoon at the Gabba, the subject of the impish Sid Barnes came up. What was the truth behind his Test ban in the early 1950s? Bill paused, gave a half-amused sideways look, and said: "You seem to forget I was an Australian selector at the time." I said I knew that "but it was fifty years ago!" All I got was a "Yes, well..."

At his lovely home in north Brisbane it was no easier. He would gladly talk about any cricketer who came to mind, but only in a kindly way. My

W.A.Brown in the Lord's press-box just on 60 years after he had made a Test hundred at the ground and 55 years after scoring 206 not out there (Australia's 100th century against England)

probing seemed too much for him at one point: "Why don't we have a dip in the pool?"

But I had not gone all that way just to swim or drown in Billy Brown's pool. So he found the scrapbooks, which inspired further questions and further bland responses. Who left a smelly goat in Don Bradman's room during the Derbyshire match? A chuckle, a slightly embarrassed allusion to Hassett, and what seemed like a flicker of a blush when I brought up Bill's highest score, 265 not out at Chesterfield in 1938.

Aussie elegance: Bill Brown at the crease

Brown is remembered less for his prolific scoring than for his natural grace and elegance. It is demonstrated not only in moving film but even in the famous still of him shaking Len Hutton's hand seconds after the Yorkshireman had earned the world Test record at The Oval in 1938.

But that wretched reticence remained a problem. Once, in a social setting, I was listening wide-eyed to Bill's bubbly wife as she conveyed intimate assessments of some of the 1930s cricketers. Suddenly the "recital" was cut short by his entry. "Now then, Barbara, what are you telling this fella?" There was a wry smile, but he undoubtedly meant business. So we talked about the weather.

A two-way tease occurred one night as I strolled through the notorious Kings Cross area of Sydney in search of some fruit from the kerbside stalls. And who should be queuing by a stall but W.A.Brown. "I wouldn't have expected to see you here!" he said. "Nor I you, Bill!" came my only possible return of fire. We talked about the day's play, and it seemed natural to suggest we might pop into the bar. He declined. "My wife would not approve of my coming back to the hotel with alcohol on my breath." I'll never know now whether he was being serious.

He flew with the RAAF during the war, around New Guinea and other islands north of Australia. But, of course, there was no more likelihood of gleaning details about that episode than about his cricket doings. You would have gnashed your teeth to powder had he not been such a thoroughly pleasant man.

He could be generous: "What I like about talking to you, David, is that you know what you're talking about." That, the flattering remark of a born diplomat, was extremely generous of him and cheered me no end, though I was tempted to respond with: "Yes, Bill, but when are you yourself going to start talking?"

This man of sumptuous batting achievement even remained a mystery to his own family. Barbara had shared it all since the 1930s but his grandsons were left to wonder just how good a batsman Grandpa had been. This finally created a slight crack in the Brown wall: he must have thought long and hard before asking: "Perhaps you could acquire for me a few of those old *Wisdens* so I can prove to the boys that I once played cricket?"

On course to become the first Test cricketer to live to 100, Bill Brown fell four years short. I think I know what his unblinking response at the Pearly Gates might have been when questioned as to his identity: "Former sports-shop proprietor."

Sir Neville Cardus
1888-1975
Good Days in the Sun

ONLY A precious few from cricket's passing pageant have been elevated to legendary status. One such was Neville Cardus, once if not still the patron saint of cricket writers: lyrical, widely lauded, and a compulsive fantasist. Through many a train journey to school I nursed the cosy little Hart-Davis editions of his collected essays, struggling to grasp what his intention had been in describing Charlie Macartney here as Mercutio, there as Figaro, elsewhere as D'Artagnan, Charlie Mac's every innings being "like a Queen Mab's scherzo". What? As for Wilfred Rhodes, his very name was "redolent of the Dorian Hexapolis". I sometimes wonder whether dear old Neville would have been granted a seat in today's hard-nosed press-box?

But if some of his ethereal prose was lost on that youngster, I responded eagerly to his quiet humour and sensitive longing for the past, and distinctly recall tucking some of his strange words - "leitmotiv", "shibboleth", "behemoth" - into my vocabulary vault while my playground circle, at my prompting, recited the passages of teasing Northern dialect over and over.

So, twenty years on, the imminent prospect of personal contact with Cardus caused shudders of excitement to ripple through me. He was contributing to *The Cricketer*, seemingly glad of every shilling he could make, responding courteously to my suggestions as editor. Sometimes it was a phone call, sometimes a letter. I was spellbound by his precise, flutey voice and his elegant, spidery handwriting. His contributions came in that same picturesque hand: not for him anything as industrial as a typewriter.

There were meetings, some of them decidedly sociable. At Lord's he held court in the pavilion Long Room. He had never much liked press-boxes. Propped against the sturdy oak table, a frail, bespectacled, beady-eyed figure in a double-breasted suit, he was occasionally considerate of others' needs to express themselves too. More often than not he had his back to the play, for, although he wrote good and sometimes lasting stuff about current cricketers, his soul had never quite dragged itself into the second half of the 20th Century. Ripples of delight ran through us as Cardus held forth familiarly on his imperishable heroes: Archie MacLaren, Victor Trumper, Walter Brearley, Johnny Tyldesley, Emmott Robinson, Reggie Spooner . . . .

He had been the target for some corrosive comment for spending the war years abroad: in Sydney. When I played for Paddington (Trumper's old club) in the early 1960s, Cardus was still listed as a club vice-president. Knowing that he had lived around Elizabeth Bay in the early 1940s and had even once plied his anaemic leg-breaks at Rushcutters Bay Oval enhanced my pride in playing for "Paddo". These were links that mattered for a star-struck young cricketer. Neville shared my sadness when the old club folded up.

Sir Neville Cardus, cricket's literary romantic, never entirely at home in a press-box (photo by John Woodcock)

I once toyed with the idea of writing a first in-depth biography of Trumper, and Neville readily agreed to supply a foreword. But it was not to be.

An invitation to visit him at his flat in the deceptively grandly named Bickenhall Mansions, not far from Lord's, was swiftly accepted. There the wide-ranging cricket conversation flowed. Regrettably I was incapable of offering much on his renowned twin passion, classical music. He signed those prized Hart-Davis editions, and other books such as *The Noblest Game*, which he inscribed "With my best wishes for many good days in the sun", the last five words a smart combination of two of his famous titles.

He was alert too. When I held out an alternative edition of one of his books for inscription, he hesitated. Had he not signed this one already? Perhaps he suspected that I was trying to cash in with a spare to sell later? My explanation was graciously accepted.

Our last meeting was in a steakhouse in Baker Street. A farmer in Australia had sent me an old bat and asked for the signatures of Cardus, Arlott and Swanton to be put on it. So, by arrangement, off to London I went and there sat Sir Neville, not with a cricketer at his side but a cellist – female – and aptly she came from Australia. That wispy autograph might have been the last he ever gave.

An imagined musical gathering of cricket people: Don Bradman at the piano, John Small with violin, W.G.Grace about to sing, music critic Cardus framed on the wall: a sketch by DF for The Cricketer 1973

Denis Compton
1918-1997
Joy to a Nation

MOST SCHOOLBOYS in North-West London in the late 1940s had one sporting idol: Denis Compton of Middlesex, England and Arsenal. He must have been the best-loved English sportsman of the century. The almost car-less suburban streets teemed with little Comptons, capless, full of joy, trying to clout the tennis ball away with that famous sweep shot.

Soon I found myself living on the other side of the world, and grieving over Denis's failures in the 1950-51 Ashes Tests. He averaged 7.57. I saw him bowl his left-arm spinners in the Sydney Test; asked him for the first of so many times for his autograph at, of all events, a speedway meeting; and spotted him again during my autograph watch outside the Hotel Australia. It was there that this careworn schoolboy observed the Compton walk, an insouciant, rolling gait, and decided to copy it. It

The stroke for which he was world-famous: the sweep

bespoke carefree confidence. Soon my schoolmates were asking whether I'd ruptured my ankles.

Four years later the game's best-loved player made a nice 84 in the Test match at the SCG after an uneasy start. I can vividly recapture how he suddenly liberated himself from the frustration by tossing his unfamiliar cap over to the umpire. A more relaxed and recognisable Denis was soon sweeping and driving like the superstar we knew.

It was some years before I saw him again, as a fellow inmate of the press-box. Through the 1960s to the '80s he was a popular, ever-broadening figure, his smiling eyes and boyish chuckle always a life-enhancing feature of what was then a star-studded gallery.

On a few occasions I was surprised to see the companionable Compo quite fired up: once when someone unwittingly took his newspaper, and then at a press conference where he gave England captain Tony Greig a grilling. Greig threatened to leave the room. This was the same uncompromising side of Denis that had powered him, bareheaded and without thigh-pad, through stirring hundreds against the ferocity of Lindwall and Miller.

I always seemed to be asking him for signatures in books and on photographs and unfailingly he wrote warm inscriptions. As he signed that glorious picture of himself leaving the field at Hastings after his record 17th century of that legendary 1947 summer, he mused not about that historic innings but about the lovely girl he met that evening.

In Barbados, on a Wisden tour in the 1980s, he was superb value, chatting patiently and animatedly with the tourists, the peals of laughter precious symptoms of his warm nature. Nor was he vain: he splashed in the water

Relaxed in later years: Compton with Trevor Bailey, Don Wilson and their ladies, Barbados 1981

with a global stomach flopping over his swim-trunks, the surgical scar across that infamous, bothersome knee plainly visible.

In the 1990s, having gathered together film from his glory years, we invited him to the annual cricket film show at the NFT. He was mobbed as he hobbled down the aisle. There was one particularly piquant moment. On the huge silver screen, the Compton of 1947 and 1948 drove and cut and swept and grinned. The now-ageing heartthrob of the masses, looking up from the front row, had his eyes fixed hypnotically and moistly on those images of his young self. He was no longer in the audience with us. He was back in that happy, uncomplicated time just after the war, when cricket was something to be revelled in to the full by the people and the players alike, for they knew the real meaning of life.

They named a stand after Denis at his beloved Lord's, but it's somewhat sad that his ashes were scattered on the turf there because years later that turf was dug up and replaced during the installation of a new drainage system. I wish I'd known. There would have been a very welcome home on my lawn for Denis Compton, the man who brought true joy to a nation.

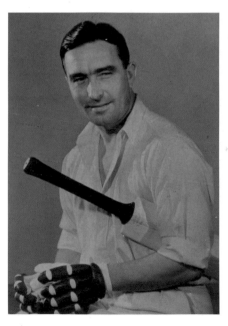

The formal and charismatic Denis Compton

Lord Colin Cowdrey
1932-2000
A Politician's Guardedness

THERE WAS the smooth, well-fleshed young England batsman who, in partnership with Peter May, swung the Ashes Test at Sydney in December 1954. And there was the same chap down by the pickets at third man at the end of the series, flannels crumpled, expansive waistline now more obvious. He had a crinkly smile and a slightly Boris Johnson distracted manner. As a member of an ABC Radio audience I'd watched him giggle his way through an interview. When questioned about his future after Oxford, he said something about making tea for the directors of a department store.

Sometimes at sea: young Cowdrey photographed on deck in 1954 by John Woodcock

Who then might have predicted that Colin Cowdrey, England's exquisite 22-year-old batting star, the "new Hammond", would go on to play 114 Tests and score 107 first-class hundreds, move into banking public relations and the ICC presidency . . . and one day become Baron Cowdrey of Tonbridge, CBE? Baron Cowdrey!

Bill O'Reilly, who knew about these things, cautioned that you "never get thanked for peeing on statues". Well, here goes. I'm afraid the puzzle over whether Cowdrey, as England captain, truly did support D'Oliveira's selection for the 1968-69 tour of South Africa was not the only instance of suspected manoeuvres behind the scenes.

A problem in 1974 began with a discreet enquiry from Sir Don Bradman about finding a replacement for Australia's representative at ICC meetings in London. I sounded out Colin Cowdrey. He seemed excited at the prospect. But in the days before emails, words travelled slowly around the world. By the time my airletter reached Don in Adelaide it had been decided to appoint John Warr. Cowdrey was clearly disappointed, and probably felt that I'd muddled the matter. There was mutual embarrassment.

The next significant contact came nearly 20 years later when Sir Don wondered if Wisden's owner, Paul Getty jnr, might like to finance the next stage of the Bradman Museum in Bowral, New South Wales. Optimistically, I said I would gladly tender the request. The request and its follow-up received no response.

One evening Don rang. He said that Colin Cowdrey saw Paul quite often and would take up the cause: "He gave me to understand he was virtually Getty's financial adviser." I was to step aside and leave the matter with him now. Colin rang and reiterated the plan, asking me rather firmly to keep well clear. Weeks passed, and Don's letters conveyed impatience: apparently Denis Compton was now going to approach Getty since Cowdrey was, in Compo's words to Bradman, "unreliable". Why didn't I ring Cowdrey re Getty? So I did, urging a response from Getty's secretary. Didn't I know? Know what? That the potential benefactor had turned down the request. *"English* cricket needs all the help it can get!" explained the billionaire when next I saw him.

Meanwhile, Colin Cowdrey, unable to deliver good news to Don Bradman, had vanished into the night. It just remained for the "messenger" to be "shot". Don was none too pleased. "A week's pocket money from Getty would be a nice gesture to recognise Australia." I seem to have created the impression that the donation was a certainty. It was presumably just a question of how much. Our friendship survived, but I was left wondering about those behind-scenes manoeuvres. Next

With Kent manager Les Ames the day Kent won the County Championship at The Oval in 1970

time I saw dear old Colin he gave me that benign smile.

Maybe, like most things, it doesn't really matter. Not now anyway. Numerous cricketers upon closer acquaintance have disappointed. Colin was said to have suffered sleepless nights simply worrying about what to do should he win the toss. Peter May would evaluate a match situation by saying: "If we add another 150 here . . ." whereas Cowdrey would tend to visualise losing three quick wickets. When he chose, however, he could be firm. In 1973, at a meeting at *The Cricketer*, approval was being sought for an artist's paintings of six famous players. "You can burn this one of me!" said Colin. No diplomacy there.

He was innately courteous, and always generous with his signature and his time, but beneath that endearing chubbiness, that ever-ready smile, gentle handshake, ready chuckle – perhaps an auto-chuckle – there was a politician's guardedness, part of an acute faculty for calculation and assessment of all people and things. Maybe this very animal shrewdness was a key component in his success as a batsman, for which all who saw him bat were grateful: because he truly had an ease of strokeplay that was God-given.

The smoothest drive in Christendom:
M.C.Cowdrey in full flow

Bob Crisp
1911-1994
Man Who Did Almost Everything

NEVER HAVE I met a more fascinating cricketer than R.J.Crisp of Rhodesia, Western Province, Worcestershire and South Africa. On the 1935 tour of England his robust fast bowling reaped him 107 first-class wickets (at 19.58), 34 of them in May – almost one for every woman with whom he was associated that summer, according to his son. Having had a spell of 5 for 0 at Worcester, he played a part in the first South African Test victory on English soil when they won at Lord's, and he took 5 for 99 at Old Trafford, where the great Hammond was a scalp, as he was to be again at Gezira in a wartime match.

Bob Crisp played at home against Australia in 1935-36 but his Test career ended there, merrily signed off with four ducks. Settling in England for a time, he bagged hosts of wickets for Sir Julien Cahn's private team, then played a few county matches in 1938 (7 for 82 against Middlesex at Lord's) before injury intervened. Crisp had once taken nine wickets in an innings for Western Province at Durban and eight against Griqualand West. Add that he remains the only bowler twice to have taken four wickets in four balls – as well as a four-in-five – and you have one truly stunning cricketer.

In 1935: Bob Crisp at his cricketing peak

Yet this was only half of it, for Bob Crisp served heroically in the Royal Tank Regiment. After the evacuation from Greece in 1941 he faced even more vicious German shell-fire in the Western Desert. He led from the front and had six tanks – four in one lucky day – blasted from under him by enemy fire. Wounded and much decorated, he almost died when shrapnel pierced his skull, that same shell killing a comrade.

General Auchinleck had signed his immediate DSO recommendation and later, with Crisp now a major, the new commander-in-chief of Middle East Forces, General Alexander (Harrow XI, 1910), endorsed a bar to the DSO, only for Field Marshal Montgomery (St Pauls, 1905-06) to convert it down to a Military Cross. Crisp wrote two lively books on his wartime escapades in the dunes, the text typically colourful and finely observed. He explained his courage as simply "a reaction to the shame I felt at being afraid", and his crooning in the nightclubs of Alexandria contrasted with the claustrophobic horrors of tank warfare.

In the 1970s, diagnosed with cancer, he sailed his small boat around the Greek islands, again refusing to die, with red wine endorsing that refusal. Almost by the way, he had also beaten the American world champion in a 110-yard hurdle race in his youth, climbed Mount Kilimanjaro twice in a fortnight, and swum naked across Loch Lomond. His life made Keith Miller's seem pedestrian.

Crisp in 1989, with a life of astounding achievement almost complete

Imagine, then, the quiver of excitement when, at Randburg during the 1989 gathering of cricketers from several countries and generations during South Africa's Test centenary celebrations, I asked someone to identify that tall white-haired chap with a goatee beard, scholarly in horn-rimmed glasses, radiating a presence during this historic first-ever match between black and white schoolboys. Thus began a treasured association with Bob Crisp, man of the world.

He had founded a South African newspaper for the black population and pursued an intermittent career in journalism with a spell in Fleet Street. He readily agreed, over a drink, to write for *Wisden Cricket Monthly*. Predictably he pulled no punches. I liked his no-nonsense approach, although a few readers took exception. It was simply R.J.Crisp, now in print, alternating bouncers and yorkers with honest conviction.

The former South African premier (Vorster), who was involved in the exclusion of Cape coloured Basil D'Oliveira from England's 1968-69 touring team, "would not have known the difference between cover point and a condom". Now (1989), international pressure to go on ignoring the multiracial progress made by the South African cricket authorities stemmed from "ignorance and blackmail".

Interestingly, Bob Crisp felt that a peaceful future as a nation lay in a federation of semi-autonomous states, black and white: "Nothing else is feasible." He had been "startled" by the integration of all races into the cricket programme, and lived just long enough to see South Africa belatedly welcomed back into the international fold. Their players of today would surely be inspired by a study of the life of that colourful forerunner R.J.Crisp.

The action that brought him four wickets
in four balls (twice)

Bill Edrich
1916-1986
What Did You Do in the War?

ON AUGUST 12, 1941, Flight Lieutenant (soon to be Squadron Leader) W.J.Edrich took off from RAF Massingham with his formation of six Blenheim light bombers on a perilous low-level raid on power stations in the Ruhr. Although twelve of the 54 aircraft were shot down, the operation was successful, and this daring exploit earned Middlesex and England cricketer Edrich the DFC (Distinguished Flying Cross).

Meanwhile, at our north London home, aged four and a half and intermittently terrified, I was doing my best to comfort my trembling mother in the damp, musty, candle-lit air-raid shelter in the garden as the nightly terrors continued to thunder and rage all around us. We regularly prayed that my brave fireman father would survive yet another night dealing with the death and destruction inflicted on London by the German Heinkels and Dorniers.

Forty years later, at a cocktail reception in London, that same Bill Edrich, swaying gently, launched an attack on me: "What did you do in the war then?" he asked sneeringly.

When we were Lord's Taverners team-mates: DF with Jock Livingston and Bill Edrich

I considered tendering a flippant response: "I was first ashore on Sword beach on D-Day" perhaps; or a teasing "I was a conscientious objector (what?!)." Instead, I explained my role as a desperate infant source of comfort to my poor Mum. He sniffed. He wasn't finished: "Anyway," he said, eyes half-closed, "you're a bloody rotten editor."

Aha! The truth was out: the Norfolk connection. Edrich was friendly with the proprietor of *The Cricketer*, who, having tipped me overboard a few years earlier, had not taken kindly to my starting up a better magazine called *Wisden Cricket Monthly*.

A few years previously I'd played in a Lord's Taverners match at Goodwood, proud to have W.J.Edrich as captain. That day he scored 61, one run more than his age. It was a rugged innings. Not naturally graceful, he was often very effective. There was an affectation about his batsmanship, as with his speech, and it is noticeable how close he comes to toppling over in demonstrating the forward defensive in a coaching film.

I'd watched him in a Sydney Test match in 1954-55. Misbehaviour had cost him a place on the previous tour (1950-51), and he was now past it on this one. Len Hutton, perhaps sentimentally, preferred him over Reg Simpson.

Edrich's dismissal at Sydney was not an elegant thing. He jabbed a lifter to gully off the shoulder of the bat, an image that lives still in my cluttered memory bank, along with the slip catch he held and the one which he dropped.

Fortunately there are happier images. To a then-stranger he had once light-heartedly signed books, and at a memorable Lord's Taverners celebratory dinner he shared the spotlight with the other legendary guests of honour, Keith Miller and Ray Lindwall and his inseparable Middlesex and England batting partner Denis Compton. Warmth and laughter and fraternity filled the great room. That was the Bill Edrich worth remembering.

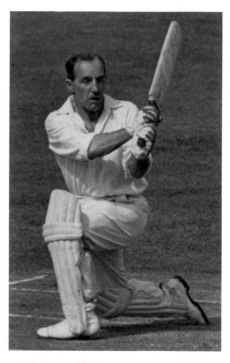

Effective without being any sort of stylist, Edrich, the RAF hero, smacks one to leg

He was the chap who went to the wicket with Len Hutton in 1938, falling early and leaving Len to go on to his famous 364. In South Africa that winter Edrich had a ghastly run of outs before showing 'em with 219 in the ten-day Test at Durban (having dispensed with abstemious early nights, which hadn't restored his form). In 1947, Compton amassed an incredible and attractive 3816 runs, and his little mate wasn't far behind with 3539. W.J.Edrich was certainly a scrapper.

Even the circumstances of his death were unconventional. He fell backwards down the stairs after returning home from a *seven-and-a-half-hour* lunch on St George's Day, 1986. Naturally, Compton, his "twin", was among those in attendance at his memorial service at St Clement Danes, central church of the RAF, as was Edrich's widow (his fifth wife). Wartime songstress Anne Shelton, who ranked alongside Vera Lynn, sang Bill's favourite, *A Nightingale Sang in Berkeley Square*. Her high heels clicked resonantly across the stone floor as she returned to her seat, and I can't have been the only one who felt a strong impulse to applaud, while brushing a tear away.

His ashes were scattered at Lord's, like Compton's eleven years later, all now lost after the returfing. Bill Edrich certainly indulged himself through life, affecting everyone within reach. And now at last I suppose I ought to forgive him.

Godfrey Evans

1920-1999

Chuckling Behind the Stumps

BAPTISMAL SIGHT of England in the field, 60 years ago, encapsulated the unique outline of wicketkeeper T.G.Evans: broad of beam, short in the leg, furry forearms, rosy cheeks as yet uncovered by the famous white whiskers of later life. Most catching was the non-stop bounce and enthusiasm of the little man from Kent, keeping the toiling bowlers going as Hassett's Australians took control at the beautiful Sydney ground.

Four years later Godfrey was back, this time as a key member of a triumphant team, leaping ecstatically to arrest Tyson's flying thunderbolts and combining with Wardle's spin wizardry to confound the Australians. Again his optimistic cries stood out. And when he emerged from the SCG pavilion that evening I had my first close-up view of that retrousse nose, small, mobile mouth, little bump of a chin, sparkling eyes. He asked if anybody had seen his wife, a role reversal, I later discovered, since she was usually the one left wondering where he was.

Godfrey hadn't looked so confident earlier, when Tyson was flattened by

Evans catches Harvey (122) off Bedser, Old Trafford 1953; he'd missed him early in his innings and was stung by the criticism

91

Lindwall, and he had to replace the groggy Englishman at the batting crease as he was finally helped from the field. No helmets then.

Years later the retired T.G.Evans became a cherished friend. In fact he was simply everybody's affable friend, a great rarity. He was always good to have around, not least as the celebrity face of the bookmakers when cricket

Genial Godfrey in mufti: a study by John Woodcock

re-opened its doors to betting. When the principal overdid the celebrating and regurgitated all his gin-and-tonics in the press-box before sliding into a deep sleep, the writers looked askance. But Godders sprang to the rescue, mopping up and cracking jokes. He reminded everyone: "I run a pub, don't forget!"

He had a charming speech oddity: everyone was greeted with "Hello, marshter!" It was a joy to hear him describe how he "shtumped" somebody. This world presented no worries – or that's what he would have had us believe. Godfrey Evans was simply great to have around. He was not glamorous in the Compton/Miller mode, but he lit up a room as he entered, and the ladies loved him for his bubbly spirit. And he loved them back.

It was something of a shock when he became serious. During discussion on the dreadful (for England) Ashes tour of 1958-59, he surprised me by saying that manager F.R.Brown wanted to lodge an early official protest about Australia's chucker fast bowlers but was overruled by skipper P.B.H.May. Most of us thought that *nobody* ever overruled FRB.

Then, during an otherwise happy lunch at Arundel, Godfrey revealed a long-lasting grievance. He once missed a catch off Neil Harvey from a nick off Brian Statham. The ball took him by surprise as it continued its upward curve from the bat's edge. Evans's gloves were the wrong way round and the ball crashed into his collarbone. A certain commentator, he was told, had been unforgiving in his judgment, not comprehending the technical nicety of the error, and had gone on about it. It still hurt all these years later. Tears of a clown.

Yet he could laugh off the worst day of his career, when he blundered several times behind the stumps as Australia amazed the world by hitting off the 404 needed on the final day at Headingley in 1948. A further regret was that he never caught or stumped Don Bradman in their 14 matches in opposition. The painful understory was that he *did* once catch him, but the umpire pointed out later that he hadn't appealed.

Nor was he bitter at having been denied – by India's delaying tactics – a century before lunch in the 1952 Lord's Test. And he was sharp enough, when accepting a figurine of himself, to identify instantly the catch on which it was modelled: "Ken Funston, Johannesburg, 1957!"

At his 70th birthday bash he was

Godfrey Evans: ever ready to perform, ever ready to chuckle

bouncing around like a 20-year-old. Soon he was forced to heed a warning to avoid gin-and-tonic – but not for long. Then he was gone, and I closed his obituary by saying how tempting it was to subscribe to a belief in reincarnation. Ah well, I have his 1954-55 tour blazer in my museum. A smile is called for – it's a *duty* – whenever I catch sight of it.

Percy Fender
1892-1985
A 1921 Reverse Sweep

TOM WEBSTER'S famous 1920s caricatures of P.G.H.Fender became internationally renowned: the Chaplin moustache, sweater stretching down to his knees, the air of rampant eccentricity. As a bowler Fender could produce just about any trick in the book. As a batsman he scored what remains the fastest first-class century in a genuine match situation. As a theorist Fender had some input into Bodyline in pre-tour discussion in 1932 with his friend and successor as Surrey captain Douglas Jardine. Yet he himself never captained England, which was puzzling. The all-powerful Lord Harris's disapproval was the underlying cause. For one thing, PGH seemed too keen to bring amateurs and professionals together.

The prospect of meeting him was exciting. The venue was his dimly-lit office in Mayfair's Balfour Mews, where he ran his wine business. Although

P.G.H.Fender, as innovative a player and captain as English cricket has known

close to 80, "Percy George", slightly stooped, chin receding, seemed hardly to have altered from the long, lean shape of the pre-war years.

His answers to the flow of questions were thoughtful, perhaps at first restrained by suspicion. Might I be one of those tabloid people? (*The Times* accurately described his speech as "circumlocutory".) Asked about his 1920-21 tour of Australia, he recalled with a pained look the captain's remarks as they sailed down the Channel, only a few hours out of England. Leaning on the ship's railing, J.W.H.T.Douglas told him that he did not rate his batting and did not think much of his bowling either. "I asked, 'Why was I selected then?' I thought I might as well jump off the ship and swim home."

England were whitewashed in 1920-21, and Fender is remembered more for his acerbic newspaper comments that caused an ugly crowd reaction. He played in the last three Tests and did well, though on his debut, at Adelaide, he dropped a difficult chance off Charlie Kelleway, on nought, when England had been easing into a good position. It became an indelible blot as the Australian batted for seven hours.

As for Fender's famous record 35-minute century for Surrey at Northampton in 1920, he said it might have come even faster. Fearing that the declaration would come with his hundred, he actually eased off so that "Podgy" Peach could reach his double-century first. PGH confirmed his memory of it in a later letter: "When Peach got his 200, I was 99 and taking the first ball of

Blind and almost alone with his memories, Fender entertains a visit from the author and keeps out the cold with his First World War flying jacket

the next over. At the end of that over I had scored 24 more." From that pre-computer age it is impossible to be certain about many things. Surrey's scorebook was carelessly lost years ago and Northamptonshire's is confusing where it matters.

In March 1977 PGH was the oldest Englishman present at the great Test Centenary gathering in Melbourne. Now almost completely blind, he had his grandson Nick with him: "He is my eyes," he said, with a proud smile.

A letter written by PGH around that time reveals a courageous indifference to the mis-spelling caused by an inability to see the keyboard clearly: a friend "us hoing to drive me up to the Oval for yje Yrst, amd. I hopr, rnablr ,r to tevive some of those ,e,ories anf, prthspd, to meet some old Friends there". It's a nice test of a reader's intelligence.

Percy Fender hoped not to disgrace himself by tumbling down those pavilion steps he had known so well.

When I saw him for the last time, he was living with his daughter in West Sussex. We sat in the rich sunlight of an autumn afternoon. He wore his First World War flying jacket (he served in both world wars) and was clearly worn out by his 90 years of life. His sight had gone completely, but not his memory. Dick Streeton had just written a superb biography, and he signed the title page semi-legibly in felt-tip, this old gentleman who had played the reverse sweep against Armstrong's negative leg theory way back in 1921 and taken four wickets and suffered two dropped catches all in one over at Lord's. One of his firm beliefs was that "a captain's first duty is to be calm, cool and collected". Most days throw up examples of this. Fender's way is the pathway to success.

Jack Fingleton
1908-1981
Seldom a Passive Moment

THERE CAN never have been a touchier cricketer than Jack Fingleton, nor one more interesting to talk to. Sitting with him through that extraordinary Oval Test match of 1968 was as good as having *Cricket Crisis* and *Brightly Fades the Don* read to you by the author himself, with rich asides.

Fingo had strong opinions about everything and nursed a few grievances too. The most painful of these was the blame he endured for the leaking of Bill Woodfull's famous outburst at Adelaide Oval during the Bodyline series of 1932-33. He reckoned it cost him the 1934 tour of England. Looking at me through heavy-lidded eyes, he growled that it was none other than Don Bradman who had passed on the Australian captain's outraged utterance to a reporter. But I must never breathe a word of this as long as Jack lived. No chance.

So it was surprising to find him splashing the story himself a few years later. His feud with Bradman (with whom he once shared a match-swinging Ashes stand of 346) was not because of religion or freemasonry. It stemmed simply from a clash of personalities.

Fingo's touchiness had been evident during his Test career (he staged a sit-down protest at Trent Bridge in 1938) and in his later broadcasting. "We? Who's we?" he exploded when BBC Bill Frindall murmured that "we" (i.e. England) needed to score at 3.68 an over to

The Fingleton hook: he was brave against Bodyline and prolific in South Africa

win. Good point, but perhaps made rather too emphatically for *Test Match Special's* tastes. When he was playfully ribbed for his pair of ducks in the Adelaide Test of the Bodyline series there was no laughing shrug. He simply punched straight back with the statement that he was the first man to score four consecutive hundreds in Test history. G'donya, Fingo!

I liked, too, his explanation about averting Harold Larwood's more

The Jack Fingleton of the 1930s, keen to joke but surely as touchy then as later

fearsome delivery – not the bouncer but the 100mph late outswinger. Jack prodded the pitch at the halfway mark, angering the bowler, who then let fly with a stream of bumpers. The hideous peppering Fingleton took from Bill Voce during a brave hundred for New South Wales stressed his mother so greatly that she vowed she would never again watch him bat.

In 1971 Fingo lined up a job for me with the Australian News Bureau, and was understandably put out when I soon quit. Then I wrote in *The Cricketer* that Harold Larwood told me that it was Fingleton's 1948 newspaper speculation that the great old fast bowler was considering leaving his Blackpool sweet shop and emigrating to Australia that got him thinking seriously about it. The word "mischievous" offended Jack, who imagined his professional integrity tarnished and demanded an apology. When I resisted, he turned to E.W.Swanton, the magazine's editorial director. "Now look heah, David," pleaded EWS, "I find myself rather like the ham in the sandwich." I pointed out that I felt likewise – between Larwood's innocent assertion and Fingleton's furious denial.

Eventually an appeasement was printed. The painful upshot was that Fingo ignored me now whenever we were in the same room.

The stand-off was eventually defused in a most peculiar way. He was umpiring in the cricket writers' "Ashes Test" at Harrogate in 1977, in which Kerry Packer played. Ian Chappell had a bowl, and Jack made history by launching into a cluster of melodramatic calls and signals following his first ball: no-ball, wide, byes, as well as warnings for running on the pitch and abusing the umpire. It was hilarious. Then he turned towards mid-on, where I happened to be standing, and delivered himself of a friendly wink.

Later I found myself in a fruitful partnership with Ian Chappell, and it was comforting next morning in the press-box to behold Jack Fingleton ease himself into his seat, look across and say in a loud whisper: "Cover-drive Frith!"

Mates once more.

George Geary

1893-1981

Caught Just in Time

KEEN CRICKET fans know that the best first-class analysis ever recorded is Hedley Verity's 10 for 10 for Yorkshire v Nottinghamshire in 1932. Fewer could name the previous record-holder. At Pontypridd in 1929, George Geary took 10 for 18 for his native Leicestershire against Glamorgan. And in 1973, when he was in his 80th year, I tracked him down.

Tall and genial, he welcomed me into the home where he lived alone with his memories and his albums, his faded England cap hanging from the framed photograph of Geary shaking King George V's hand in the 1934 line-up at Lord's – his final Test match.

He was now a widower, but 10 of his 15 brothers and sisters were still living. His thoughts were locked into the past for much of each day. A yeoman bowler, he used to cut the ball at brisk pace and was so controlled that even with Woodfull, Jackson, Kippax, Ryder and Bradman at the crease at Melbourne in the last of the 1928-29 Test matches, George had bowled 81 six-ball overs, taking five wickets for only 105 runs, then wheeling down 20 more overs in the second innings of this eight-day Test match. "There's nobody

How tempus fugits: Geary the reminiscent old man

ever bowled as many in Australia," he mused proudly.

Geary hit the winner in the third Test, when most of the players hid in the lavatory while England chased down 332 to win by three wickets. "I never got excited," he said. He sold that bat for £10. "Jack Hobbs told me I'd have got £250 for it in London: the bat that won the Ashes!"

Nor was that the only time he was centre-stage as the Ashes were won. That distinction had come his way in 1926, when he sealed a famous victory at The Oval by bowling Arthur Mailey. England's win then triggered the sort of English euphoria seen in 2005. The two slip catches Geary held off Larwood caused such bruising to the *backs* of his hands that he could scarcely feel the ball when he bowled. And there was an even more painful memory: only hours before England's triumph "someone got into the bedroom [of the hotel] and pinched all my money!"

That 1926 Ashes series was paramount among his crowded memories. What of Arthur Carr's infamous error at slip fifth ball of the Headingley match, Macartney going on to crack a pre-lunch hundred? "I'm afraid his [Carr's] remarks would be unprintable!" Geary helped save that Test, resisting stoutly with George Macaulay (108 for the ninth wicket) – almost avoiding the follow-on.

George made a pot of tea, reflecting further on his long, rewarding career, with a tangible

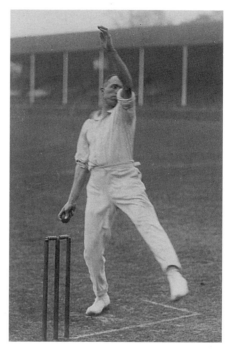

George Geary, once the world record-holder with 10 for 18

sense of yearning. "Tempus certainly fugits!" he said with surprising *eclat* for a shoemaker's son. Spinning an aircraft propeller when some fool had left the switch open almost cost him his life during the First World War. The blade slashed his left shoulder and thigh. "I was black for weeks. They said I was finished with cricket. I was offered a pension of three-and-six a week."

He idolised Wally Hammond. Don Bradman? He *"meant business!"* That pitch on which he made his 334 at Headingley was "doped". The disgust George felt in 1930 reignited as he thought about it further: "Duckworth missed Bradman off me when he was 107 runs. It was an easy catch." And later George was adjudged run out for 0: "A shocking decision. Old umpire Bestwick spent the interval in the toilet."

George played his penultimate Test at Trent Bridge in 1934, when he was 40, and he scored 53 ("I could see O'Reilly set his teeth. It made me set mine."), adding 101 with Patsy Hendren to keep England in the contest after dismissing Bradman for the third time in Tests. He had also castled the greatest of all batsmen at Leicester with that evil leg-cutter, the technique which he later passed on to Alec Bedser.

He soldiered on for a few more seasons, having a second benefit at Leicester (£10 being his princely return from the match at Hinckley) then coaching for 20 years at Charterhouse, where there was nothing he could teach the brilliant schoolboy Peter May.

It was very warming to be in George Geary's company. I had to drag myself away. A few years later I sought him out again. Now in a nursing-home, he wore a fixed smile, but his eyes were vacant. Dementia had taken its terrible, or merciful, grip. I'd got him to share his memories only just in time.

Paul Gibb

1913-1977

Mystical, Forgotten Record-Breaker

IT HAD those of us who were in the know suppressing giggles. This man with a toupe was parading himself in front of Trevor Bailey and Doug Insole at the mass gathering of old Ashes cricketers in Melbourne during the Test Centenary delebrations. They had absolutely no idea that it was their old Essex team-mate Paul Gibb. He had lost most of his hair when young, so the familiar figure who played for England either side of the Second World War was a rare bald player. This way and then that passed this bewigged chap with teasing smile, until his two old colleagues became slightly worried about this odd little intruder. Then he introduced himself, and everyone fell about laughing.

Gibb cuts during his extraordinary Test debut: 93 and 106 at Johannesburg, Christmas week 1938

I had heard that he was driving a bus around Guildford. The transport manager introduced us, and a series of enjoyable chats began. Gibb's name is seldom mentioned today but his record is quite startling, at least to begin with. After a debut hundred for Yorkshire in 1935 (against Larwood and Voce), he was selected in 1938 for the washed-out Old Trafford Test against Australia. That Christmas, on Test debut as an England opener, he laboured his way to 93 and 106 at Johannesburg. A 58 in the next Test, opening with Len Hutton, preceded a patient 120 (then the slowest Test century: 451 minutes) at Durban, where he shared a record stand of 280 with Bill Edrich. England famously finished on 654 for 5 on the tenth day, 42 short of victory when they had to hurry off to catch the ship home.

Against India in the first post-war Tests, Gibb kept wicket and made some runs, and he went to Australia as keeper in 1946-47. But after playing (in sun-hat) in the Brisbane Test, his health uncertain, he made way for the ebullient showman Godfrey Evans, who became England's busy, buoyant gloveman for the next 12 years. After a break from the game Gibb had some very successful

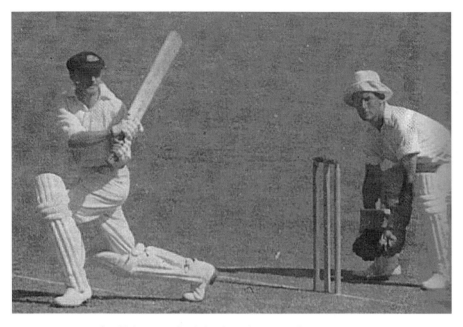

Paul Gibb keeps wicket behind Bradman, Brisbane Test 1946-47

years with Essex, then became the first Oxbridge Blue to work as a county umpire (he called Tony Lock, Harold Rhodes and Butch White for throwing), journeying around in a camper-van. Then he drifted into obscurity.

He was good company, if rather shy and reticent. Reminiscences came haltingly. I suggested some sittings with the tape recorder. He agreed at length but only if I was willing to do the interview while he drove his bus down the country lanes of Surrey. The background noise would be a problem but I seized at the offer. First, though, he had to consider the invitation to the 1977 Melbourne Centenary Test. He was reluctant, fearful of the inevitable crowds. Due to leave two days after the body of former players, I encouraged him to go and offered to drive him to the airport.

So, "trapped" in my car, he responded to the probing, and I began to see into his troubled mind. He simply did not know where he belonged. He revealed that he had flown Sunderlands for Coastal Command during the war, which left him standing on cricket fields after the war wondering what the devil he was doing there. What was the point of it all? His marriage failed and he lost track of his two sons.

After the great Melbourne party, and his little joke with Insole and Bailey, he returned to his bus duties. Soon I would be recording his memories. Then came the phone call. It was the manager. Paul had reported for duty that morning, collapsed and died. So that recording was never to be.

We traced one of his sons, who later allowed me to serialise Gibb's tour diaries in *Wisden Cricket Monthly*.

Gibb and family: sadly later to split up

They were frank and fascinating and people speak of them still: the obsession with ice cream and with clouds ("ten-tenths layer of altostratus" – a throwback to his war in the air), his confession that he was bored when surrounded by strangers "unless I have a good deal to drink". And as England's keeper in the Brisbane Test, when Bradman (on 28) was given not out to that edge to second slip, he had one of the best views: Out! The Don went on to 187, shaping the course of post-war cricket, leaving the serious Paul Gibb to lament that "the umpire was either unwilling or afraid to give a decision against a man of so high an authority in the Australian cricket world".

Eddie Gilbert
c1905-1978
Back from the Dead

IT WAS the most unlikely encounter of them all, simply because the Queensland cricket community was agreed that the old cricketer I was trying to track down had been dead for years. Days of painstaking investigation had revealed only one clue: Eddie Gilbert, the legendary and popular Aboriginal express bowler of the 1930s, had finished his days at a security unit west of Brisbane. So I went there, expecting at last to establish the date of death for cricket's records.

The superintendent grudgingly revealed that Eddie had been admitted in 1949, a sick man, an alcoholic, who had treated his wife badly. But exactly when had he died? After a few more evasive comments the man's tone became clear: he was speaking of Eddie Gilbert in the present tense. "Surely he's not here now, is he?" Indeed he was. Then I must see him!

"I'm sorry. I can't do that. It wouldn't be any use. Eddie doesn't speak. We've tried everything: put a cricket ball in his hand, he just stared at it, let it fall to the ground." The poor old cricketer was in a bad way, quite heavily sedated.

A picture of Eddie Gilbert which supports the view that he chucked

He had been a sensation in the 1930s, causing Don Bradman to finish up on the seat of his pants, then having him caught behind for a famous duck. The Don stated that it was the fastest spurt of bowling he ever experienced. Many other batsmen from bush, grade and state cricket gave similar testimony.

But some contemporaries doubted the legality of his fastest ball, respected writer Ray Robinson among them: "Eddie was too obviously a chucker, with no approach that could be called a run-up, just three or four walking steps." It was assumed that the boomerang-throwing action had been turned into a lethal bowling catapult. New South Wales cricketer Bill Hunt was another who condemned Eddie's action: "He came in at Number 11 and just for fun I knocked his stumps over with a deliberate chuck. He put his arm round me and laughed. He said, 'That was a beauty!' So ya see, the little bugger couldn't tell a bowl from a throw!"

Gilbert was no-balled in a Shield match, although today it's assumed that colour prejudice alone kept him out of the Australian XI. Yet, having raised Australian spirits by hurting England's aloof captain Douglas Jardine in Queensland's match against the tourists, Eddie Gilbert bowled in the nets with the Australian team before the Bodyline Test at the Gabba, and had been listed by the Board among the Test possibilities. There was no colour bar.

Frustratingly, there did seem to be an official bar to my seeing him now, and I was resigned to leaving Goodna. Then my wife mentioned that her father used to work at the mental hospital down the road. The superintendent stirred. He remembered "Sonny", and away they went down Memory Lane. I sat quietly. When the time seemed right I repeated my plea to be allowed to meet the legend. The man in charge picked up the phone and said: "Find Eddie."

My heart thumped as the minutes ticked by. His black locks now silver, long arms dangling by his frail frame, the once-famous little black fast bowler stood at the doorway. His handshake was feeble. Having accepted a cigarette, he stared fixedly at the floor. There was no response to some gentle questioning. He just quietly wheezed, head slowly rocking.

"Would he sign his name for me?"

"I doubt it."

He was given a ballpoint. After an agonised minute he dropped it and shuffled backwards. That "E" that he managed to scrawl I now value as

Found at last: Gilbert in the asylum

highly as any other autograph.

At last he looked up. His deep-set, bloodshot eyes sent a shiver through Debbie as they met hers. "Thanks, Eddie," said the boss. And the old fast bowler shuffled through the doorway, out into the harsh sunlight and across the parched ground.

He died six years later. Alzheimer's was discreetly entered as cause of death. Years later a decent headstone was placed on his grave at the Cherbourg Aboriginal settlement. In terms of curiosity, pathos and fanciful myth, Eddie Gilbert has a truly unique place in cricket's long history.

Fun with fellow Queenslanders: Gilbert with boomerang

Arthur Gilligan
1894-1976
Tales from the 'Twenties

ARTHUR GILLIGAN was a living fragment of the halcyon 1920s Ashes Test matches, a hearty chap in a tweed jacket who still addressed everyone as "old boy". His friendliness had once radiated as a cricket broadcaster, and, before that, as a Cambridge, Sussex and England fast-bowling amateur allrounder and captain.

And now he was a willing captive in my car as we motored across the land to a dinner in Somerset. It was some privilege to have him all to myself, with his willingness to spin a fascinating yarn about almost any player from the 1920s onwards.

During an earlier visit to his home in Pulborough, Sussex I was struck by his powers of recollection. The sound tapes rapidly filled. It was not easy adjusting to the world of 1974 after those hours of memory-tapping. This man had even been present as a seven-year-old at the classic 1902 Oval Test, watching his hero Victor Trumper (oddly with no retrospective mention of the blazing centurymaker Gilbert Jessop).

Like almost everybody else who played against Warwick Armstrong, Gilligan had a derogatory tale to relate: Arthur bowled, the lumbering Australian took a run, bashed into him, and said gratuitously: "D'ya think I did that on purpose?"

"I had the great pleasure of knocking his cap off next ball," said Gilligan, with a pantomime evil grin.

Adelaide, 1924-25, and England's defeat by 11 runs on the seventh day: "I blame myself," he said gallantly. He was caught by his pal Vic Richardson at cover off Jack Gregory's slower ball. The bowler told him that the ball had slipped. He

Tossing with Australia's skipper Herbie Collins during the 1924-25 series

also counselled Gilligan on how to combat fatigue when bowling eight-ball overs on a stinking hot day: you simply bowled two wider ones at medium pace off a shortened run.

Together Gilligan and Maurice Tate had bowled South Africa out at Edgbaston for 30 the previous summer, the ball seaming everywhere. A different sensation came with an outburst by Lancashire's talented rebel Cec Parkin concerning Gilligan's leadership. MCC's termination of Parkin's Test career left Arthur sad: "Parkin was jolly good fun. I was very fond of him. He wrote me a charming letter afterwards and told me he was 'a bit sozzled one night' and a pressman quoted something he said."

Later in life, a gentleman of Pulborough, Sussex

Having given me his brother Harold's address (another England captain from the Charleston years, and father-in-law of Peter May: I called on him shortly afterwards) Arthur dipped again into his rich storehouse of memories. He said he had scored hundreds from every position from No.6 to 11. The century at No.10 was in a Gentlemen v Players match at The Oval in 1924, following a nasty blow over the heart. At 98, Tate, his jovial county bowling partner, hinted that a "gimme" was on its way. The ball dipped on leg stump and whistled past off stump. "You've got a pal, haven't you?" murmured Herbert Strudwick, the little wicketkeeper.

The hundred came through a deliberate misfield by "Podgy" Peach. "When we next played Surrey," Arthur recalled, "I gave him a full toss to get him off the mark." Chivalry was alive in those days.

Tea and toasted crumpets; then a committee-room secret slipped out: the sacking of Arthur Carr in 1926 had been followed by a free-for-all over his replacement for the decisive Oval Test match. Gilligan, now the sole survivor from that gathering, recalled that Plum Warner erred in allowing Carr to remain in the room to vote on his successor as England captain. Jack Hobbs broke the deadlock by switching his vote to Percy Chapman. "The meeting lasted six hours. But Carr should not have been in that room." And then the Ashes were won, amid rare jubilation. Such is the inner history.

Arthur had served as MCC president and was now Sussex president. I was driving him to Bath for the Lansdown CC 150th anniversary dinner at the historic Assembly Rooms. There the inimitable speechmaker Alan Gibson play-acted, pretending to have spotted the ghosts of certain famous old cricketers up in the gallery alcoves: "And up there I see Arthur Gilligan too … Oh dear, no, Arthur's still here with us, of course."

If only that were still so. And if only the misanthropic zealot responsible for all but expunging Arthur's name from the developed Hove ground of today realised what a disgraceful slur this is.

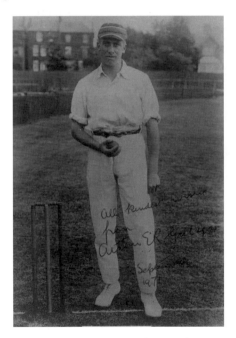

A.E.R.Gilligan, archetypical
English gentleman cricketer between
the world wars

Alf Gover
1908-2001
Leap Year Man

"GOVER'S" WAS a cosy meeting-place, happily remembered by all its many patrons. Test cricketers, club cricketers, fathers and sons would descend on the unpretentious premises in Wandsworth, south-west London, for coaching and conviviality. The tall, presiding figure was Alfred Gover of Surrey and England, fast bowler, journalist, raconteur and renowned coach.

Oddly enough, although he took 1555 first-class wickets, Gover is remembered as much as anything for his coaching and his friendly cricket school in Wandsworth

Alf had played big cricket from 1928 to 1947. He took 200 wickets in 1936 and again in 1937, rare performances for a fast man. Often he joked ruefully about the countless catches dropped off him by his Surrey slips fieldsmen. He would stand by the canvas walls of the net, an imposing presence in England sweater (three Tests before the war, one after), elegant white cravat at his throat, assuring a keen father that his youngster – propping forward mechanically, leading elbow impeccably high – might well have a future, and

112

that a further course of lessons might help.

His approach was conventional, and I often wondered if someone like Jeff Thomson, with his slightly unorthodox action, might have been coached into obscurity. But, as my son firmly told me, you don't argue about that sort of thing with a man wearing the crown and three lions. Years later I came across film of Alf Gover in action. He was all knees and elbows. Yet another instance of doing as I say, not as I do.

In adjacent nets the genial Australian John McMahon would be making the lads feel comfortable and the great Arthur Wellard would be rolling an arm over. There is poignant recall of old Arthur dragging his feet up East Hill, returning to the nets after his lunchtime pint, drab raincoat hanging from drooping shoulders which had once powered some of the mightiest hits the game has seen. Casual passers-by were not to know that.

An hour in the nets at Gover's left you gasping for breath. There was an oxygen deficiency in there. The gas heaters were blamed. Fresh air was to be found down in the shop or over in the bar, where Alf (he sometimes seemed to prefer "Alfred") held court, and the fun

Alfred Gover, one of the best fast bowlers of his time, though seldom capped by his country

began. He specialised in pre-war reminiscence: tales of extraordinary matches and personalities, and easy repeats of his most familiar story: that run-up in a match in India which didn't culminate in release of the ball. Propelled by the dire effects of dysentery, he continued sprinting all the way up to the dressing-room. Captain Lionel Tennyson was soon bellowing into the cubicle for Alf to let them have the ball back so the game could proceed.

He sometimes joked about his list of the greatest womanisers in the pre-war game, a certain Essex player securing the ultimate nomination. Then he would pay solemn tribute to the immortals, Jack Hobbs and Percy Fender paramount among them. The snooker table beckoned, pre-payment needed per frame of course. Action and team photos hanging from the club-room walls sparked further chat.

Gover's brother-in-law Eddie Watts had a sports shop over in Cheam. I played alongside him when he was in his fifties. He was also easy-going and kindly, a true man of his time. He had taken all 10 against Warwickshire in 1939. I bought a bat for £2 from Eddie, and later he sold me his exquisite run of *Scores and Biographies*.

When Alf became Surrey president in 1980 he became a symbol of welcome at the humble old Oval, at a time when the club had a soul. "Meet Monty Garland-Wells . . . Tom Barling . . . Stuart Surridge . . ." The committee-room introductions were a delight for one who had known these cricketers only as names in *Wisden*. "Now, old boy, would you care for a red or white?"

In 1991 he produced a lively autobiography. It was strewn with mis-spellings, but he took the critical review well and inscribed my copy "With all kindest regards". Or perhaps he signed the book before he saw the review? Anyway, by then he was too old to bounce me.

Alf Gover's eternal joke was his birthday. He was that rarity: a Leap Year baby (February 29, 1908). Even now he would have been celebrating only 26 birthdays. If only.

Jack Gregory
1895-1973
Tracking Down a Recluse

IT WAS a crazy risk to leap into the car and drive non-stop for over three hours down the scenic New South Wales coast road one morning in 1972 just in the off-chance of finding Jack Gregory.

Jack Gregory, maker of the fastest Test century: no cap, no gloves; did he even bother with a "box"?

He had been the world's most dynamic cricketer in the 1920s, a dashing pin-up of an allrounder. Two Test records remain his to this day: the fastest hundred in terms of time (70 minutes, at the old Wanderers ground, Johannesburg, in 1921) and most catches by a fieldsman in a series (15, standing amazingly close at slip in that whitewash over England in 1920-21, when this ultimate allrounder also took 23 wickets and hammered 442 runs at 73).

Having served in the First Australian Imperial Force on the Western Front, Gregory terrorised England and the counties with his thunderbolts on two tours in the 1920s, married a Miss Australia, broke down at Brisbane's Exhibition Ground during Don Bradman's first Test, and then just about disappeared from view, a widower and recluse who fished and played bowls, attracting the description "cricket's Garbo".

His replies to my letters in 1971 were courteous, but he flatly refused any kind of interview. The reason emerged: when Charlie Kelleway was omitted from the 1926 tour of England, a pressman asked Jack what he thought about it. "Blowed if I know," he said innocently. This throwaway line materialised in print next day as: "Jack Gregory can't understand why Kelleway was omitted." The Board gave him a hard time over that. Consequence: a determination never to speak to anybody from the media ever again. "You will find plenty of old cricketers who may like to talk about their deeds in the past, but I am sorry I cannot do the same," he wrote.

My clever plan was to race down to Narooma and innocently ask him to sign some books on the 1920s Ashes series. Who knows? A conversation might ensue. So finely balanced was my luck that day that had I stopped for petrol I would just have missed him.

It would be an exaggeration to say that I got a warm welcome from this tall, white-haired 76-year-old, but I made it into the kitchen, where he signed the books. The television was still on, providing a distraction (President Nixon had just landed in China). I slipped in a casual question or two. Jack Gregory liked the new limited-overs form of cricket because, as he'd said in a letter: "I loved the game and liked to hit hard, and also I tried to amuse the public, who like to see bright cricket."

J. M. GREGORY.

Arthur Mailey's attempt at portraying Gregory's ferocity with the new ball

He not only batted bare-headed but without gloves too. It's not known if he wore a protective box. I'd seen the absence of gloves and headwear on film, but sensed it might prompt an early descent down the steps of his modest shack if I suggested that this had been a foolhardy practice.

Surely it wouldn't upset him if I brought up that 70-minute Test century? He said he hadn't realised it was a record until his son mentioned it some time later. Jack even got the minutes wrong, believing it was 75. But at least we were now chatting away like old pals. He remarked on the local fishing: "Caught six bream yesterday. A friend landed a nine-pound flathead this morning." He also played bowls.

Then he touched upon his ancestry, which stretched back to the early days of white settlement in Australia. He was proud to belong to a great Australian cricket clan, seven of whom played first-class cricket, four of them in Tests.

A strong smell of liniment hung in the air. "My knee's like a barometer. I had to put some of that stuff on. It's going to rain soon." We chatted some more. I still could scarcely believe my luck. Then he stood up, and I knew my time was up. Had I dared to produce a tape-recorder or a notepad I know I would have been dispatched head-first down those steps.

I took my leave of this great old cricketer with one final liberty: wanting a photograph, I clicked the shutter before he could refuse. With that I drove to the nearby beach and scribbled down his words while they still echoed in my head. I can hear some of them still as I reflect on one of the most productive gambles of my life.

A quick snap, probably the last-ever, of Australia's entertaining all-rounder of the 1920s

Tony Greig
1946-2012
Generous Giant

FIRST SIGHTING was memorable: Lord's, 1968, President of MCC's XI versus the Australians. He was so tall that he actually seemed out of place on that field, the bright golden hair emphasising his uniqueness. Could this Greig chap really play? He did little wrong that day and took a couple of wickets. My two blond-haired sons were so smitten that they scampered after him into the Tavern that evening, and he smilingly signed their scorecards. That was the man we came to know so well: enthusiasm personified.

Never too busy to sign for fans, Greig always gave legible signatures

In the early 1970s only one South African had played Test cricket for England and that was Basil D'Oliveira, whose story became emotional legend. Tony Greig had a Scottish father who had flown with Bomber Command in the Second World War, but with South Africa now outlawed from international cricket indefinitely there was good reason for anyone born in that benighted land to try his luck in England, particularly if he had British ancestry. By 1975, when Mike Denness's captaincy came to a jolting end, Greig, having won his first Test cap in 1972 (making two half-centuries, just like Kevin Pietersen in 2005), was just the man. The sight of him, legs seemingly twenty feet long, leaping through the gate and onto the Lord's turf, with his players racing on behind him as the lads over by the Tavern croaked *Rule Britannia*, was an experience never to be forgotten.

"Greigy's" approach was gung-ho and highly welcome after the duffing-up England had been given in Australia by Lillee and Thomson. He was back in Sydney for the 1975-76 season, and while he was there I had a letter from my father (long resident in Sydney) saying that he'd like to send my late mother's diamond ring to us in England but was worried about the risk of loss in the post. Any ideas? I wrote back to say that I'd got to know Tony Greig pretty well in social settings as well as press conferences. He might be worth a try. Dad got in touch, and the England captain said that if he met him at Sydney airport at a particular time he'd gladly carry out the mission.

Some weeks later I had a call from Greig to say he was in Brighton, he had the ring with him, and I'd better get down there quick smart. To this day I wonder how many other Test cricketers would be willing to perform such a favour.

We sat in the empty Hove ground in pale spring sunshine, and after taking possession of the ring and trying to express my gratitude adequately, I enjoyed a personal account of the '75-76 season in Australia. He chuckled as he recalled the apparent reluctance of new West Indies batsman Vivian Richards to leave the Gabba dressing-room when it was his turn to bat. (Richards made 0 and 12, but came good in the last two Tests – and dominated thereafter until his

retirement 15 years later.) Greigy had seen Richards' shaky baptism at close quarters, and very soon after handing over the ring he was telling the world that he and his England players would be making the West Indians "grovel". There has probably been no more indiscreet public utterance in the history of Test cricket.

After the outcry, and for years to come, Tony Greig kept on apologising, and always with a chuckle. It was hard to think of anything that might get him down for long.

A marked man now, he failed in four of the five 1976 Tests, but had enough character to give public penance at The Oval, crawling on his

The highest honour: captain of England: Greig on the players' balcony at Lord's with Chris Old and Bob Woolmer in 1976

hands and knees for the world to see: with a bright smile, of course. Within months he had taken India by storm. Then came revelation of the Packer set-up, an upheaval of gigantic dimension. How did one approach him now? Hadn't he betrayed the game? His zestful salesmanship swept aside much of the reservation. He himself was now set up financially, and top cricketers everywhere were about to be well rewarded, in stark contrast to their past modest earnings.

At Melbourne's VFL Park, under primitive floodlights and with hardly any spectators, he was in his most avuncular mood as he explained how this bizarre new form of loud and colourful international cricket would sweep away the existing feudal system. Hard as it was to endure the growing brashness and cacophony of World Series Cricket, had we but known it, it was here to stay, lighting the touchpaper of cricket's money mania which has inflated with every passing year.

As if that wasn't enough, Greig was let loose on TV commentary for years to come. Depending on one's current mood, this could be either irritating or hilarious. But still there was nothing personal. Most of us could never dislike the man. You find out the truth when someone dies, and the sense of loss reached the furthest boundaries of the cricket world.

Another proud moment: Tony Greig introduces his players to Her Majesty the Queen

George Headley
1909-1983
A Laugh over Hot Chilli

WHILE GEORGE Headley was often referred to as the Black Bradman, the Caribbean preference was always for Don Bradman to be called the White Headley. Statistics strongly support Headley's lofty repute: first-class average nearly 70; Test average 60; 10 centuries in 22 Tests; twin hundreds against England at Georgetown and also at Lord's. This diminutive champion carried West Indies batting on his shoulders through the pre-war decade, earning the name "Atlas". West Indies' first black captain in 1948 ("It wasn't altogether a popular appointment"), Headley would have held the post longer had he been born later.

Now, in 1981, at the Kensington Oval in Barbados, he was among the veterans of 53 years of West Indies Test cricket, from Teddy Hoad of the 1928 series and Derek Sealy, who played at 17 alongside Headley in the very first Test in the Caribbean (1930), through to the current all-conquering force led by Clive Lloyd. West Indies were playing England and Headley was besieged. Of all those available his was the autograph most eagerly sought. Apart from the autographs, our conversation was interrupted only by thunderous roars as one of the West Indies quicks took another wicket or hammered flesh. When England suffered an obviously dodgy lbw, the old master's reaction was one of spontaneous alarm and sympathy: "Oh no! That spoils my day."

With an equally renowned West Indies cricketer, Learie Constantine

My day could not be spoiled. In a deep, smoky voice George Headley talked fondly of England, where his playing days finished in the leagues and his son Ron was a Worcestershire player who won a couple of West Indies Test caps. (How proud George would have been had he lived to see his grandson Dean bowling for England.)

Back to the early days – the pioneering tour of Australia in 1930-31, when spinner Clarrie Grimmett was a problem. George gripped my arm and rocked with laughter as he recalled being stumped at Adelaide. He didn't bother mentioning the Brisbane century or another at Sydney that set up West Indies' first Test victory away from home.

Suddenly he was serious, recalling that one member of that 1930-31 side (which had needed special clearance through Australia's then repressive immigration/passport laws) declared himself as "European" on the customs document when this was not quite the case. George himself had written "African".

George Headley was a batting phenomenon

Having seen film of Headley in action was helpful. While few glimpses survive in the conventional newsreel archives, among the reels of amateur footage shot at Trent Bridge in the 1930s there are lengthy sequences of George Headley at the crease. He was seldom still: exceptional footwork, bat not always conventionally straight but moving fast, like a rapier: there is a rare sense of electric animation about that small, scuttling figure. Similarities with Bradman are marked.

He enjoyed an enduring friendship with The Don, who years later gave me a letter written to him by Headley from Jamaica, expressing his concern at the lack of team spirit in the 1975-76 West Indies side. He need not have worried. This was soon to be put right.

What was about to go seriously wrong was lunch. We sat in the pavilion, he courteously getting to his feet every few minutes to accept handshakes and sign some object or other. Yes, he might well have worn a helmet if they'd been around then. He certainly saw the cricket bat as an implement of attack rather than defence.

Then he noticed my poised spoonful of hot chilli sauce. There was urgency in his deep blue eyes as he warned me against it. I halved the dose, and it was still lethal. As my lips burned and tears spilled, his chuckle expanded to full-blown hilarity.

I'm glad I was able to give back some small entertainment in return for his memorable company.

That hot chilli sauce is about to take its toll, reducing the great Headley to helpless laughter

Hunter Hendry
1895-1988
A Moaner with Talent

"BY GEE, Dye-v'd," roared "Stork" Hendry, gazing up at the high vaulting of Guildford Cathedral. "This is a bloody lovely church!" We were the only visitors to England's youngest cathedral, but the verger was nearby and he had the good grace to smile benignly on his colonial visitor.

H. L. HENDRY.

"Stork" Hendry as seen by his team-mate Arthur Mailey

It was 1975 and H.S.T.L.Hendry, capped 11 times by Australia in the 1920s, was on his first visit to England for 49 years. He had been deeply upset at being denied entry to the Long Room at Lord's: "You'll find me in the photos of the Australian teams of 1921 and 1926 hanging on your walls," he piped at the steward. And when the VIP hospitality at "the Home of Cricket" proved inferior to that which had recently been laid on for English guests at the MCG, he complained to Gubby Allen.

Don Bradman, in a letter, had labelled Hendry "a moaner" whose career record had been very ordinary. In one of Hendry's letters Bradman was described as "anything but popular in Sydney" after "having left NSW high and dry" in 1934. So there was no love lost between two part-contemporaries.

Hendry's last Test series, 1928-29, was The Don's first, and he faded out after Adelaide, when Archie Jackson made his glorious 164 on debut. Hendry had made his sole century for Australia two Tests earlier, adding 215 with Bill Woodfull at Sydney. That hot summer saw Hendry and Wally Hammond (905 runs in the five Tests) passing each other in the field hundreds of times, and it was Hendry's abiding memory that a peculiar smell emanated from the great England batsman, like none he had ever known elsewhere: not the usual "natural" perspiration odour of sportsmen. It seems now, in view of revelations which came too late to enlighten Hendry, that the whiffs were probably a consequence of the mercury treatment Hammond was undergoing after the illness he contracted in the West Indies a couple of years before.

Hendry could play all right: he once hit 325 not out for Victoria against the New Zealanders; and over Christmas 1926 he contributed 100 to Victoria's total of 1107 against New South Wales, when Arthur Mailey kept having catches dropped by spectators in the outer.

M.A.Noble, young Hendry's Paddington club captain, seeing the tall, gangling slip fielder with legs crossed, had named him "Stork", but he made it clear that he preferred "Hunter". Friendly and opinionated – Frank Sinatra was "a mongrel", and with pumpkins 70c a pound, the world was in "an awful mess" – recalled his attempt to comfort D.R.Jardine when the aloof Englishman, on his first tour of Australia, was being barracked. Jardine rewarded him with the assertion that Australians were "uneducated and an unruly mob". Hendry blinked before telling the future Bodyline leader that, all right then, he could "go to buggery".

Hendry on his visit to Guildford: "bloody lovely church!"

Later that summer drinks were taken when Hendry was 96 in the second Test. Patsy Hendren alerted him that his had been spiked. Stork defiantly swigged it, then clouted Hammond for four to raise his hundred.

He and wife Vida invited me to dinner at their Sydney harbourside home. There was little to be seen by way of memorabilia apart from a gold medallion given at Trent Bridge to each member of the 1921 Australian team by the great F.R.Spofforth to mark the 100th England v Australia Test match. Hendry was now planning that pilgrimage to England, but had to postpone it when his shares plunged. But he and his diminutive wife eventually made it, and he gradually overcame his shock at what had happened to London, spotting something familiar at last: Simpson's-in-the-Strand, where the teams of the 1920s had been entertained.

I got him to write for *The Cricketer*, an opportunity he utilised to unburden himself of much criticism of the modern game. But for me the supreme delight was to play against once of Armstrong's mighty 1921 side, albeit with a tennis ball on the back lawn.

Towards the end he found himself Australia's senior Test survivor, and the generations were bridged through a friendship with Steve Waugh. It was a mercy that Hunter Hendry was spared many subsequent developments in cricket that would have given him apoplexy.

Bill Hunt
1908-1983
Archie Jackson's Mate

SO WHO the devil was Bill Hunt? Well, for a start, he was separated from the vast majority of mankind by having played Test cricket for Australia. Admittedly it was only the once, against South Africa at Adelaide in 1931-32, the match in which Don Bradman was left stranded on 299 not out. Bill registered a duck at No.9 and, following O'Reilly and Grimmett at the bowling crease, took 0 for 25 and 0 for 14. Then he was dropped: simply because virtuous captain Bill Woodfull objected to his flow of ripe language. Bill was adamant about that.

Caricature of Hunt which cannot recapture his drawling and caustic bandinage

Elsewhere he was truly a force to be reckoned with: in first-grade and Sheffield Shield cricket and for Rishton in the Lancashire League (9 for 62 against Accrington on one occasion). His slow left-armers claimed hat-tricks galore, and it was easy to imagine how his chitchat would have worn down umpires and opposing batsmen. The only thing that ever truly upset him, he said in a voice every bit as nasal as Shane Warne's, "was the mug umpires I had to contend with". They were seemingly on Bill's side the afternoon he took all 10 Paddington wickets for 55, including Alan McGilvray (b.Hunt 7), while the wondrous Arthur Mailey took 0 for 30 off 15 overs at the other end. That evening Bill tore the page from the scorebook and took it home as a souvenir.

When I set out to write a biography of Don Bradman's elegant contemporary

Archie Jackson, who died in 1933 at the age of 23, everyone I spoke to in Sydney's cricket fraternity said: "You must see Bill Hunt." Bill and Archie had been boys together in the 1920s in the industrial suburb of Balmain, and Bill was very close to that slender, charming hero right up to his death in 1933. He simply worshipped his memory, and was understandably very possessive about his tragic mate. This man turned out to be the most vital link with my subject.

He took me to see Archie Jackson's imposing gravestone at the Field of Mars cemetery, and showed me letters from him. The anecdotes and general recall poured forth. The bonanza was a rare short film of Archie demonstrating his strokes.

The trouble started when the book took a little longer to complete than I'd anticipated, and Bill became understandably impatient. He had been very supportive: "Rest assured I can always supply the answers." But his impatience intensified to the point where an October 1973 letter contained a challenge: "If you would like me to take over from you I will gladly do so, as I still feel you have left so much left to be said that to my way of thinking is still unsaid."

Bill Hunt has a chuckle with Learie Constantine after the mighty West Indian had belted him out of the Sydney Cricket Ground

Bill went further: "By the way my friend after viewing your photo action [in *The Cricketer*] in the nets it disgusted me to say the least. Your delivery action so cramped and unbalanced to say the least you must bowl like an octopus not with any fluency and poetry of motion like a Mailey or Grimmett." I guess that's just one reason why I never rose to Test level, as Bill had done.

I was now well aware that he had always been argumentative by nature, but his letters became steadily more irascible and impatient, until he announced that he now intended to write the Archie Jackson book himself. It would take him two years and would be called *The Doc, Arthur, Archie and I*, which would at least have acknowledged the support and patronage given to the two impoverished Balmain youths by Labor politician H.V.Evatt and Arthur Mailey.

On unrelated matters, never one to shy away from exaggeration, Bill condemned the hype which enveloped young Sydney batsman Ian Davis, who was tagged by one journalist as the "new Archie Jackson": "There is such a wide gap between his bat and pads," raged Bill, "I could drive a double-decker bus through it."

Still he kept the pressure on this struggling author. In another airmail letter and in his finest Ernie Wise style he pushed me further: "Hows about that rubbish you have wrote the manuscript evidently you are not game to let me read it or don't you trust me with it. I only wanted to make a great number of corrections for you."

I could easily imagine how his "banter" as a bowler must have annoyed batsmen in Australia and North-West England. I wonder what he said to Learie Constantine after that West Indies whirlwind had hit him out of the Sydney Cricket Ground and into the neighbouring Showground?

When at long last I was able – not without a certain trepidation – to send Bill a finished copy of *The Archie Jackson Story* in 1974, he calmed down. By then, writing was difficult for him, so he sent the odd tape recording. These must be the only record on Earth of the voice of this disputatious yet somehow likeable man.

Hunt by the grave of his beloved young pal Archie Jackson

Sir Len Hutton
1916-1990
All Balance and Poise

IT SEEMS rather pitiful now. I would sit in the school classroom day upon day with forefinger pressed firmly against nose, hoping to reshape it to resemble that of the finest batsman in the world, Len Hutton. His silky leg glance, his exquisite cover-drive, his balance and poise, all seen on the newsreels and eventually in the flesh at the SCG, were the peak of my aspirations. What chance was there that I might one day be able to bat like Hutton as well as bowl like Lindwall?

Then there was that fine suit that the Yorkshireman wore on the 1954-55 tour: pale blue, neatly cut. I searched through the shops of Sydney for something like it, but it must have been obtainable only over in Bradford.

I'd watched him bat in Canberra in 1950-51 and in the newsreels of the dramatic Ashes series of 1953, then "live" again in the two Sydney Tests of '54-55. Midst a torrid duel with Lindwall he memorably back-cut to the pickets high over slip. Then, in his final Ashes Test, he fell for 6, glancing a pre-arranged Lindwall inswinger to Burge. Len finished that match by bowling Benaud, a strange and memorable final ball in a drawn Test which sealed a valiant and glorious 17-year Ashes career.

Padding up yet again: Len Hutton, devoted to batting, often suffering in the cause

Schoolboys like me tended to drift into a trance at the very thought of Hutton's 364 against Australia at The Oval in 1938. He was 22, and he batted for *797 minutes*. Of all cricket's stats, this remained the most awesome. And that magical aura lasted through the years until, fine in that blue suit, he was approached yet again for his autograph.

During the 1970s and 1980s a precious acquaintance developed. He was present at most of the major matches and cricket functions, seldom initiating conversation but always polite in response, occasionally eager, sometimes a little sardonic. The restrained non-committal expression used in battle against Lindwall and Miller, Rowan and Mann, Ramadhin and Valentine served him in everyday life. He was quiet, some said wise, others that his mind was often merely on other matters. Always he had seemed weighed down by his cricket responsibilities and by life's vicissitudes. I sympathised.

In 1988, having agreed to be filmed at Headingley for a video programme I was making on "Golden Great" bowlers, he spoke with amusing and masterful understatement about the perils of facing O'Reilly and Miller. A few days later he telephoned to ask if the £50 cash fee was really all that was available. I could but chuckle. Ray Lindwall had murmured that he'd have done it for nothing. If it had been in my remit I would have paid them each £50,000.

At home in Kingston-upon-Thames, Len sat beside a bookshelf housing the *Wisdens* which precisely covered his career: 1935 edition up to 1956. I'd brought some Ashes tour books for signature, and as each was opened he enquired after the author, all of whom he'd known well. How's Lyn Wellings? Arthritis, not at all well. John Arlott? Big lung problem. Ian Peebles? Oh dear: all the depressing news seemed to make Len flinch. So I said Peebles this summer looked fit enough to bowl 30 overs.

The cares of his playing days behind him, Sir Len has donned another of those neatly-cut suits. Picture by John Woodcock

Yorkshire's cricket fraternity gave their hallowed son a gala celebration in Leeds in 1988 for the 50th anniversary of that 364, with many contemporaries from England and Australia present. Although he sometimes radiated something close to regret at the burdensome legacy that awesome Test innings had placed on his slender young shoulders, on this night those alert eyes glistened at the sight of his nimble young self on the screen during that famous 1938 marathon. He signed many menus and things and was, by his standards, quite animated.

The last encounter was only a couple of weeks before he died. He looked Dresden-china delicate by now. It was at yet another dinner, and I begged for one final autograph on the menu. I was tempted to ask whether he'd still got that pale blue suit and might he like to dispose of it?

Even now I sometimes catch myself sitting at my desk with finger pressed hard against nose.

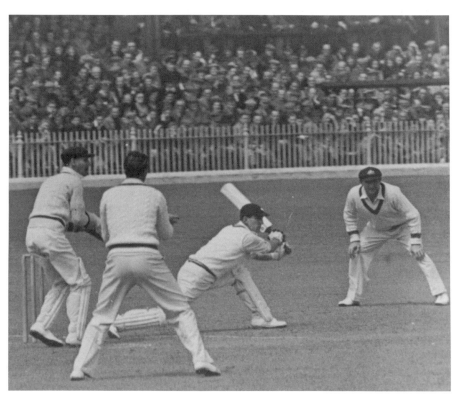

The Hutton cover-drive, which a generation of boys and men tried to emulate

Bill Johnston
1922-2007
Trunkful of Memories and Laughter

HE TRULY was the jolliest of men, laughing and chattering, notwithstanding injuries and life's setbacks, of which Bill Johnston had his share. In the 1950s he would sign autograph books and pass happy pleasantries. In the 1980s he was still chuckling, except when watching cricket on television, when some of the play and some of the commentary irritated him. Perhaps, like so many cricketers, he was longing to be back out there in the middle again.

He lived with the slightly irritating reality that the celebrated 1948 Australian tour of England continues to be remembered almost solely for Don Bradman and the fast attack: when people parrot "Lindwall and Miller" they commit a serious oversight, for while Ray Lindwall took 27 wickets in the Tests and Keith Miller just 13, the lanky, balding Bill Johnston, with his brisk, accurate, left-arm variations of inswing and outswing, took 27 – same as Lindwall – in those five Tests. He also passed 100 wickets in first-class matches on the tour, the last Aussie to do so. Yet he remains largely and cruelly close to being forgotten. If only vivid film of his bouncing, rubbery, slightly comical action were available for Mitchell Johnson to see, he would scarcely believe his eyes at the way Bill controlled the ball.

On the next tour of England, in 1953, Bill badly injured his ankle in the one-day picnic match at East Molesey at the start. This possibly cost Australia the Ashes. But he did at least go on to make hilarious history by averaging 102 for the tour in first-class cricket, somehow avoiding dismissal in 16 of his 17 innings from his natural No.11 position in the order. When I bought that bat off him he pointed to the tape near the bottom: "Look at the cracks down the inside edge. Don said that's a mark of class!"

Not all that long ago we were sharing happy times together on Queensland's Gold Coast, where this Victorian and his wife had retired. Sweet, serene Judy served afternoon tea by the side of the little pool. Frank Tyson and Ron Archer were sometimes there, and the 1950s would be relived, and in full colour. The sensational Melbourne Test of 1951-52 often came up. I was among the thousands who sat trembling by the wireless as Bill and his mate Doug Ring snicked and belted 38 for the tenth wicket to beat West Indies at the MCG, their laughter and bare-faced impudence contrasting with the

The fast bowler so grievously half-forgotten: the wondrous Bill Johnston

panicking fieldsmen.

Bill was modest, but was quietly pleased at his successes against Denis Compton in particular, whom he dismissed nine times in Tests. He was persuaded to bring out his old scrapbooks, and the columns of yellowing text and the pictures triggered memories galore. He always sought the funny side. I reminded him of Johnny Wardle's tailend assault on him in a Sydney Test, when England twice mounted decent tenth-wicket resistance in a match which they won by only 38 runs. Bill ripped down ball after ball, Wardle slashed, and the bowler's eyes followed the ball as it crashed into the midwicket pickets; then he scratched his head and laughed. "Miller kept coming over and giving me advice. Useless!" Latterday laughter.

He took early wickets in that Test in England's second innings, when

Australia looked like winning. Then, as they chased 223 for victory, Tyson reduced them to 145 for nine, at which point Bill joined Neil Harvey for a last-wicket stand which had the Englishmen worried. Harvey was all class and Bill was all heaves and swishes, and they got to within 39 of their target when Tyson had Bill caught down the leg side by Evans. Even now Mr

The difficult bit: retrieving the clothes and implements from a long-ago Test career

W.A.Johnston seemed to find that funny.

Several times I'd suggested to him that after many years of neglect those old cabin-trunks full of memorabilia out in the garage ought to be examined. Judy agreed. So the lid creaked open, and silverfish and a cockroach scrambled for their lives. Judy was close to tears. I was distraught. Bill just stared in amazement. There were the sacred 1948 cap and blazer, punctured with moth-bites. There were the menus and letters and more cuttings, far from pristine. An old Test sweater had stood no chance.

He took the relics out piece by piece, and what was worth retrieving was sold or given away. No point leaving them to rot in that trunk. But part of dear old Bill went with each of those relics – happily to two or three collectors who will preserve and cherish.

Soon afterwards Judy died; Bill moved south; and the laughter faded away.

Brian Johnston
1912-1994
"I've never seen this chap in my life"

WITH HIS jovial broadcasting and genial presence, Brian Johnston was one of cricket's favourite and legendary figures. Laughter was his gift to the world. He was good to have around. I admired him for his chuckling approach to almost every situation, but most of all because he had earned a Military Cross while serving with the Guards Armoured Division, a decoration not only for bravery but for his unrelenting cheerfulness in horrific battlefield situations as the Allies pushed into Germany in 1945.

"Johnners" centrestage, where he felt so at home, conducting the 1970-71 England players in their rather flat victory song after their triumph under Ray Illingworth in Australia

So it was tough to be told by "Johnners" in 1977 that a review I had written (embodying the critical verdict of "trite, trite, trite") of a cricket novel was "not the sort of thing we have in *The Cricketer*". I thought that a bit ripe. There was I, putting 60 or 70 hours a week into producing the magazine singlehanded in my dining-room, while he was merely a friend of the proprietor. "The sort of thing *we* have . . ."? I beg your pardon, Mr J?

He'd already displayed the caring side of his nature in 1972 when organising the Cricket Writers' Club spring dinner for the visiting Australian team. I'd just returned to England from Sydney, and was keen to attend, but all seats had been sold. So Brian took my telephone number. On the morning of the dinner, at the Skinners' Hall, London, he rang to offer me a place since one of the Aussies, an unknown named Bob Massie, wasn't well. I greatly enjoyed the meal and John Arlott's speech, and to this day, if I can steel myself sufficiently, I can still picture Ian Chappell's purple suit.

Over the years I bumped into Johnners regularly, at Test matches here and around the world, social gatherings, book launches, his honking laughter lifting all occasions. But I remained unhappy about that remark of his: "not the sort of thing *we* have . . ." Well, I imagine he wasn't too distraught at my departure from *The Cricketer* in 1978, and a gulf opened up when a serious challenge to "his" magazine presented itself a year later when *Wisden Cricket Monthly* was born, revolutionising the cosy cricket magazine industry.

We remained on friendly terms, though we now seldom spoke at length. Things cooled further when I ran a feature in *WCM* by a Scottish schoolmaster which cut through all the self-satisfied guff enveloping *Test Match Special*, mocking its obsession with cakes and the occasional irrelevant waffle. Two of the commentators subsequently told me that the feature might prove beneficial, though I doubt that BJ saw it that way.

And then one afternoon at a Test match at Headingley, Johnners, in his light-coloured suit and "co-respondent's" brogue shoes, went for one of his promenades along the concourse in front of the football stand. The fans loved it, calling out and waving. And he loved it.

Unhappily for BJ, he had forgotten to take his press pass with him, and the uniformed commissionaire, a large, unsmiling Yorkshireman, refused to readmit him into the media area. I was standing at the rear of the box at the time and happened to turn around as this impasse was escalating. Johnners caught sight of me through the iron-bar gate. He perceived imminent rescue, and waved desperately. "Frithers! Frithers! Tell this chap who I am, will you?!"

I looked solemnly at the pair of combatants for some time before delivering the verdict: "I'm afraid I've never seen this chap in my life!" I told the fellow in uniform.

Johnners let out a sort of squeal – the only word for it. Then, removing

Brian Johnston during his TV commentary days: with E.W.Swanton and Peter West

tongue from cheek and perhaps recalling his efforts on my behalf over that dinner in 1972, I spoke up for him, and he was let in, ready to continue entertaining the nation, while the commissionaire muttered something about only doing his duty.

I can't fault BJ's son's judgment (in one of the countless books by or about Brian Johnston) that I was more of an Arlott man. But that doesn't mean that I didn't have a deep regard for BJ. And it so happens, upon reflective consideration, that he was right about that book review all those years ago in *The Cricketer*. I suppose one "trite" would have sufficed.

Frank Keating
1937-2013
That Mystic Smile

THE WHIMSICAL smile that almost always played across his rounded face proclaimed Frank Keating as the friendliest and least intense member of the press-box. He played with words as a man might play at random on a flute, and in this serious world his writing served as a reminder that sport should not be treated like political or military fare. He was interested in the humanity of it all, and although I tended to be regarded as a serious chap, I actually preferred Frank's company, often alongside John Arlott. Those cherished times were always lubricated by a good glass or two of something red or white. "Here's

Happy at home: Frank and Jane Keating (centre) with the Friths

to ye, m'dear!" the man in red braces would whisper.

Frank liked to tease, and therefore laid himself open to being ragged. When he dropped a simple catch off my bowling in a friendly cricket match,

I made a point of reminding him every time we met for years afterwards. That messed up his equilibrium. The only serious argument we ever had was over the South African controversy, when Frank refused to acknowledge the hypocrisy of punishing British and Australian cricketers who played and coached youngsters of all races in South Africa during the years of that benighted country's supposed isolation while all the while Britain, Australia, India and other countries were carrying on very lucrative clandestine trade with Pretoria, their governments all turning blind eyes. A fresh glass cooled matters: the mark of true friendship. We were neither of us grudge-holders.

We came close to dying together. The airliner bucked and swayed violently as the pilot tried time and again to effect a landing around midnight during a violent tropical storm over Bali. The airport lights had blown. The runway somewhere below was unlit, glimpsed only when the lightning flashed. Passengers, many of them cricket tourists, were wailing in the pitiless semi-darkness. Some gripped their arm-rests so hard they almost snapped off. We were being tossed about like bronco riders, and death seemed imminent. The pilot's quavering voice as we rocked around for another blind attempt to land in the blackness did nothing to allay our anxiety. It was now time to say goodbye to our loved ones, one final hug.

There was a big bump and rumble, a violent sway to one side and back again. We skidded slushily to a halt. Three times the shaken pilot confirmed that we were safely down. We shan't go into how this writer and his wife felt. What was of most interest was my mate Frank, across the aisle. He was seated next to a Yorkshireman, who must have been 80, and it transpired that as we taxied in, old Joe turned po-faced to the ashen, perspiring Keating and asked, "But Frank, do you really think Boycott will sign again with Yorkshire?"

Frank was off that aeroplane like a rocket and into the candle-lit duty-free area, where he bought a bottle of potent clear liquor and sank at least half of it before we resumed our flight an hour later.

He was back to his unstoppable self when we reached Adelaide. He wanted Sir Donald Bradman's phone number so he could line up an interview. He would not accept that The Don did not give interviews. The great man's defence was cast-iron: if he gave one journalist time he'd have to give time to all of them, and there would be nothing left of his own time. I tried to span the problem by saying that I would ask when I was with DGB tomorrow. But Frank could not restrain himself.

He somehow acquired that elusive telephone number, rang him, and received the predictable negative reaction. But Bradman and friends would be playing golf next day, that much Frank gleaned, so he went out to Kooyonga, tried to arrange a few minutes with the great man, was politely told this wasn't on, and so contented himself by wandering around the golf course at a safe distance. "Keats" could create a sports column out of anything.

"It's just filling space, m'dear," he used to philosophise, a world-weary assessment if ever there was one, but spot-on. The near-death experience, though, as we tried to land on that terrifying night, surely made a far more exciting story than watching Bradman play golf.

There was no nicer environment, it seemed to me, than Frank's family home in the hills near the Welsh border. There, with that eternal grin, he held gentle court, no longer playing around much with the whimsy and nostalgia that had made his columns so sought-after as he lavished them with rich adjectives, some invented. I refrained from asking if he missed his globetrotting

Keating in caricature on the jacket of one of his cheerful books on sports and sportsmen

now. After such a busy, exciting and enjoyable career, it might have touched a nerve. But folk like Frank, who trade in nostalgia and whimsy, are good to be near.

I only wish he'd returned that copy of D.H.Lawrence's *Kangaroo* which I lent him.

Alan Kippax
1897-1972
Elegance and Dignity

LIKE SEVERAL other high-class Australian batsmen of the 1920s and 1930s, Alan Kippax would be much better remembered and appreciated today had there never been a little genius named Bradman. Kippax was New South Wales captain when the young Don made his first-class debut in 1927 and was a father figure to him as well as to Archie Jackson and Stan McCabe. Two years on, he closed the NSW innings with Bradman 452 not out, leaving Queensland 770 to win. Young Bradman was said to have been none too pleased.

The old-fashioned late cut, a stock-in-trade of Kippax, passed on to his protege Archie Jackson – and revived recently by Ian Bell, much to the gratification of spectators

Kippax was for many years the State's leading Sheffield Shield run-scorer (6096 at 70: hallowed figures I need not check). Over Christmas 1928 he had a freakish 10th-wicket stand of 307 with Hal Hooker that secured the Shield for NSW. Yet it was not just the gush of runs that elevated Kippax to the highest regard. It was his particularly elegant style, the delicacy of his late cut and the ease of his hook. As surviving film proves, he was Trumper's natural successor, right down to the halfway fold of his shirt-sleeves. As a youngster he had bowled to Trumper at the SCG nets, and he worshipped him.

My own first contact with Mr A.F.Kippax was not all that lovely. Having graduated from concrete/matting pitches to turf, I called in at his Sydney sports store in Martin Place to buy my first pair of spiked boots. Next Saturday, my run-up was very heavy going: a teenager toiling through treacle. A glance at the underside of one of the boots exposed the problem: the spikes, poorly tempered, had curled up into fish-hooks. I hesitantly took the boots back. With scarcely a word, Mr Kippax replaced them.

Twenty years later I went into that shop again, not to question him further about the boots but to talk about Archie Jackson, the ill-fated 17-year-old batting genius he had taken under his wing late in 1926 and whose life I was reconstructing. This time Alan Kippax was courtesy personified, and the long conversation led to an invitation to his home in the elite harbourside suburb of Bellevue Hill.

He and wife Mabs lived with fine old furniture and art-deco ornaments. He wore a red satin smoking-jacket and his cigarette was set in an ivory holder. It was akin to being in Noel Coward's presence, though he lacked Coward's eloquence and vanity. Like so many cricket champions of old, softly spoken Kippax had little inclination to talk about himself. The first century recorded for Australia against West Indies, the 315 not out against Queensland, his two major stands with young Bradman in the 1930 Tests against England, all this was gently brushed aside.

But he was strong on Bodyline. Having suffered a serious head injury against Queensland a year earlier (he pointed to the scar), he was one of the most outspoken critics of the English bouncer onslaught that overwhelmed him and several others in 1932-33. Dropped after the first of those torrid Tests, he still made the 1934 tour of England, although he was dogged by illness and played only in the Oval Test. His career embraced 22 Test matches, with two centuries, a puzzling lack of fulfilment. His peak years had been the 1920s, and when he was stunningly omitted from the 1926 tour of England, he thought about throwing himself off the Gap (cliffs to the east of Sydney, a favourite suicide spot). Instead, he went into business in the sports store and became a wealthy man, even with the stiff competition from shops nearby run by Bert Oldfield and Stan McCabe.

When speaking of his close pal Vic Richardson, Kippax's eyes lit up. The pair were inseparable on tour: he gave the impression that they were the Douglas Fairbanks and Spencer Tracy of the cricket world, all fun, charm and sophistication. What fascinating tales were *not* divulged that evening?

In 1930 (he finished second to Bradman in the first-class tour averages), as if to emphasise his aesthetic bent, "Kippy" scored twin centuries at Hove against Sussex and then 250 there in late August 1934. The sea air perhaps carried a scent of Sydney, the familiar setting for so many of his serene batting displays.

And yet his best innings of all, he reflected, was a 68 against Bert Ironmonger and Ted McDonald on a shocking sticky at the MCG. Whatever happened to those exciting stickies?

Alan Kippax, one of the most elegant batsmen
ever produced by Australia

Jim Laker
1922-1986
An Air of Imperturbability

LISTENING THROUGH late July nights in 1956 as Jim Laker bowled himself into immortality in faraway Manchester, a young chap had no way of foretelling that one day he would become a friend. And was I the only person on the planet at that time so stupefied by that off-spinning near-miracle that a love letter to a future wife incorporated details of that freakish 19 wickets for 90?

Two years later I watched Jim bowling at the Sydney Cricket Ground. The Australians had vowed they'd make him pay for his astounding figures on favourable English surfaces. They didn't. The master offie conceded 2.5 runs per eight-ball over and his 15 mainly top-order wickets cost only 21 apiece in a series that was as dreadful for England as the recent Ashes series have been for Australia*. No wonder Laker never got over his exclusion from England's two previous tours of Australia.

Eventually I got to shake the mighty hand that had slain 46 Australians in that 1956 Ashes series. What impressed most was his general air of imperturbabilty. As Andrew Strauss and his players celebrated success I sometimes thought of Jim and giggled as I tried to imagine him bouncing up and down like a six-year-old in that victory ring. His way, in keeping with the times, was to sling his sweater over his shoulder and stroll from the field modestly, unmolested and with a kind of majesty.

No rolling on the ground or frenzied bouncing up and down: Laker has simply just finished taking 19 wickets in a Test match, and it was natural for him to stroll off the Old Trafford turf unmolested

Everywhere he went he derived great amusement from the inescapable discussion broached by cricket-lovers about his Old Trafford near-miracle, but

*2009 and 2010-11

he was also sufficiently down-to-earth to appreciate that this was no bad thing. All the same, ever comfortable in understatement, he used to reflect that "I bowled better on a marble-top in the West Indies against Weekes, Worrell and Walcott."

When *Wisden Cricket Monthly* was launched, the phlegmatic Laker actually described the concept as "quite excitin'" (his dropped "g" was a trademark).

The bowling action of a master (Paul Gibb umpiring)

His articles always arrived on time, and every couple of years he would nudgingly compare the increase in the magazine's cover price against the static nature of his modest fee. He was genial company at the editorial get-togethers, except once when he was smouldering over some imagined slight. John Arlott said "Leave him to me", and dragged him along to our gathering, where he sipped quietly and avoided denting the happy ambience.

His fatherly presence on a *WCM* tour was valued too. Leaning on the bar in the Sydney hotel and sipping pina coladas, he enchanted the group of touring fans with shrewd and amusing opinions.

He could tease. Umpiring a match at Tim Hudson's, he turned down appeal after appeal as I toiled away with my Lindwall impersonations. At lunch I said, in desperation: "*One* of those *must* have been out, Jim?" "Oh, they all were!" he said, grinning wickedly.

His presence at a February Fools charity match added much to the attraction, especially when he agreed to bowl a ceremonial over to start the event. All six balls to John Snow were on the spot, compelling careful forward defensives. Jim was then 55.

It was always a good interlude when, after a TV commentary, leaning against the rear wall of the press-box, hands thrust deep into pockets, he'd give a wink and come over and sit down for a chat, usually drily placing the

A valued (and legible) autograph as Jim Laker obliges

latest sensation into perspective.

Near the end of his life he underwent major surgery. At his Putney home he spoke of the recent burglary, when several of his cricket souvenirs were taken. Nodding towards a silver salver attached to the wall, he murmured: "Daft buggers missed that. Shone their torches and mistook it for a mirror." His indignation was well concealed.

Which is more than can be said for his scar. "They cut me right open," he murmured. "Want to see it?" I wasn't keen, but before I could opt out he had opened his dressing-gown to display a vertical wound almost as long as a cricket stump. Fortunately there was a chair behind me, for I went at the knees. Jim's mischievous little grin was the one all those departing Australian batsmen had once witnessed.

Harold Larwood
1904-1995
A Sense of Battle

MOST PEOPLE who met Harold Larwood in his later years were surprised at his slight stature. Could this possibly have been the terror bowler who propelled the ball at around 100mph with lethal accuracy, rendering opposing batsmen sick with fear? Then you noticed the sturdy shoulders, long arms, prominent nose, alert eyes, taut lips. He may have been close to 70, but these features still conveyed a sense of battle, redolent of those long-ago days when he and burly Bill Voce blasted out Nottinghamshire's and England's opponents

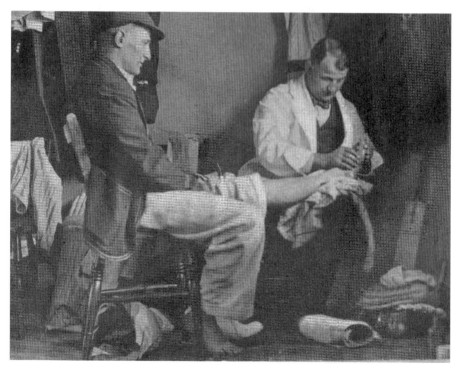

The foot damaged by his Bodyline exertions is examined

(most famously the even more diminutive Don Bradman).

Now, in the early 1970s, Larwood was an unlikely citizen of Australia. A symbol of terror as he spearheaded the Bodyline attack, he had been sent cowardly death threats during that turbulent 1932-33 Ashes series. More abuse came many years later when the wounds were reopened by an entertaining but essentially silly drama-documentary in 1984.

But the passing years had seen an amazing transition: after emigration to Australia in 1950, England's hated invader and his wife and five daughters had been warmly received by their new neighbours and workmates. Now he could sometimes even hear the crowd noise from a mile away at the Sydney Cricket Ground where, in that torrid summer of '32-33, there had been thunderous booing and hooting (followed by cheering for the 98 he smashed in the final Test).

Fortunately "Lol" was a hoarder, so the enthralling experience of looking through scrapbooks, photos and telegrams stored in boxes and suitcases took up much of the afternoon. Here were the congratulatory telegrams from the King and the MCC president which Larwood had soon been viewing with some confusion when Julien Cahn urged him after Bodyline to make a public apology for bouncing the Aussies so that England might feel free to select him again. Another was from Archie Jackson, the young Australian batsman who, from his death-bed in Brisbane, wired his congratulations to Larwood for his key role in England's Ashes victory.

Harold revered this yellowing piece of paper.

Harold Larwood's perfect action: a split-second later the ball was at the batsman's boot, stumps, gizzard or skull

Loyalty to Douglas Jardine, his captain, was evident in every reference, a rich and rare demonstration of the perfect symbiosis of one from the English upper class and one from the lower orders as they combined to bring down a common enemy. And here was that ashtray: "To Harold for the Ashes from a grateful skipper" – who had been, of course, and still was *Mr Jardine*.

Lois brought in some tea. How many pilgrims had entered that brick bungalow since the family had emigrated in 1950? How many friendly cups of tea had been served? How often, never tiring, had Harold Larwood revisited the stormy days of Bodyline and all those Test and county summers?

He didn't mind when I handled the cricket balls, most of them bearing little narrative silver shields. On the wall hung a framed photograph of the 1932-33 touring team. The majority of those cricketers were then still alive, but all are now dead.

He and his wife still spoke with something very close to their original Nottinghamshire accents as discussion ranged over scores of players and incidents. He liked this new tearaway, Lillee, but on the whole was unimpressed by current players, especially the fast bowlers: they were pampered, and he hated the hugging and kissing when a wicket fell. Had he lived beyond his 91st

In retirement in Sydney, Larwood received many visitors: this one the author's son John

year, what might Larwood have thought of central contracts, and drinks and cold towels at third man? He was already envious of the modified lbw law which allows for batsmen to be given out to balls pitched outside off stump. This, as much as the advent of Bradman, was the cause of Bodyline.

We had to laugh at his parting remark as he patted my youngster on the head and said: "Never be a fast bowler, son!" Soon afterwards he penned a warm foreword to my biography of Archie Jackson, and I saw Harold Larwood several times during the glorious Centenary Test celebrations in Melbourne in 1977. There he actually spoke for a few minutes with Don Bradman. There had been a reconciliation of sorts, though the conversation was guarded and inevitably trite. These, after all, were the most determined and uncompromising combatants in the most stirring chapter in the history of international cricket.

Frank and Harry Lee
1905-1982   1890-1981
Lee c Lee b Lee

ON PAGE 336 of the 1934 *Wisden Cricketers' Almanack* lies a curious scorecard entry for a County Championship match at Lord's. Against Somerset, the Middlesex batsman Harry Lee was caught by his brother Frank off the bowling of third brother Jack for 82. This treble entry, possibly unique, caused some hilarity, for the Lees were a warm and friendly crowd. They had all started with Middlesex. Jack and Frank then sought security with Somerset. It would have been a joy to have known them all but Jack, serving with the Pioneers, was killed in Normandy soon after the D-Day landings. He was 42.

Frank was a little younger, and Harry was the senior by some way and had served in the First World War. During the fighting at Neuve Chapelle he was reported "missing, believed dead". For three long days he lay in no-man's-land. Eventually captured, he nursed wounds that left him with a withered leg, which threatened to end his cricket. But, a batsman with the ugliest of crouches, Harry went on to make four double-centuries for Middlesex, once took 8 for 39 with offies, and played one Test match for England.

He liked to joke, but when he reflected on that emergency

Frank Lee (left) to bat with Jack Robertson

appearance for his country at the Old Wanderers, Johannesburg early in 1931, his gnarled features darkened. With injuries in the England camp, he was co-opted while coaching in South Africa. He opened with Bob Wyatt, scored 18 and 1 (exactly as Bradman had done on Test debut two years previously) and that was that. When he got back to London, Harry begged Plum Warner to give him the Test cap and blazer to which he was surely entitled, but the *eminence grise* flatly refused, mumbling something about a possible breach of

Harry Lee's coaching contract in South Africa.

As we sat and talked in Harry's flat behind Lord's, happier memories tumbled out. He recalled how the outrageous Albert Trott, the Australian who served Middlesex after his Test career was cut short, loved to hop over the rope and gulp a quick pint when a wicket fell, and how he would chew paper into soggy bullets which he'd spit at unsuspecting bystanders.

Umpire Frank Lee bends low to verify a short-leg catch by Alan Oakman off Laker's bowling, Old Trafford Test 1956

After a long and much-enjoyed playing career, making 38 centuries including five hundreds (same as Hendren and Hearne) in the famous Championship year of 1920, Harry became an umpire, soon having the rare duty of sending both his brothers on their way with leg-before decisions.

In old age Harry used to sit side-on in the old Mound Stand to watch the cricket at Lord's. After the bomb scare in 1973 there was a photo of one obstinate old man resisting police efforts to get him to move. That was Harry Lee. After his time at the Western Front he couldn't see what all the fuss was about.

Brother Frank piled up runs as a left-hander for Somerset, a favourite story being his first ball from Larwood: "I was nervous all right. That ball knocked the bat out of my hands. When I got down the other end the umpire said:

'He's a good lad, is Harold. Always gives new chaps a slower one to start.'"

But Frank will be remembered more for his umpiring. Not only was he immortalised – in his trilby hat and long white coat – by giving Jim Laker his awesome 19th wicket in that demanding 1956 Old Trafford Test but he fearlessly no-balled South Africa's Geoff Griffin for throwing in the Lord's Test of 1960, and a few others besides when the game needed such firm umpiring.

He was no exhibitionist. Calm and leisurely as he went about his serious business, Frank was one of the old brigade, and I got the feeling that if a county captain was really out he would raise his finger without fear of suffering poor marks in the captain's report. That couldn't be said of all umps in those feudal days.

Frank was the man I sought out during charity matches in the 1970s. Softly spoken, droll, twinkle in eye, gently smoking his pipe, he was a comfort to be with. As with all the old pros, his opinions were wry and sensible. They knew that a cricket life was a privilege: precious friendships, pleasant environs, a realm apart from that outside world where stress and tragedy often lurk.

The three brothers Lee: Frank, Harry and Jack

Ray Lindwall
1921-1996
Chauffeur to Chauffeur

INESCAPABLE HERO-worship shapes this memoir. Ray Lindwall was a rarity: a superstar without a trace of ego. The most-feared fast bowler of the post-war decade (matched occasionally by Keith Miller), he had the ordinary demeanour of "the chap next door". After a blitzing spell for Australia in a Test match he'd take his sweater, get his shirt collar in a tangle and, face flushed, slap his baggy green back on, shrugging modestly at his team-mates' compliments. Whether or not "Lindy" was the greatest quickie of them all, what is beyond doubt is that, just like England's Brian Statham of that breed, there has never been a nicer fellow.

Spellbound by his rhythmic, rolling, seventeen-pace approach to the crease, the distinctive uncoiling of the arm, and the explosive release, I tried relentlessly to replicate that action. I was not alone. The suburban streets of Sydney were sprinkled with young Lindwall lookalikes.

Ray Lindwall: the climax of a rhythmic, pleasing – even thrilling – action

Then, one evening by the SCG pavilion exit during a Test match in 1951, I acquired his elegant autograph. Aware that he lived two suburbs beyond my parents' house, I then mustered the courage to ask him for a lift home. "Sure," he said. Just like that. It had been a long, patient wait, for he and Arthur Morris and a couple of others had had a lot of body fluid to replace at the bar in that elegant 1880s-built pavilion: no "warming down" in those uncomplicated days.

As the car purred around the rim of Botany Bay I hoped that a tyre might burst, giving me more time in my hero's company. Not that Ray was responding all that lucidly to my probes about how he'd got the better of Stollmeyer or Weekes. He pointed across the bay to Kurnell and talked of Captain Cook, then digressed onto other matters, such as the pleasure of his tour of England. A self-effacing champion was simply unwinding.

Understandably I became a little possessive about Ray Lindwall. I was playing in the lower ranks of his club, St George, and when we bowled Randwick out for 52 (England's total in the 1948 Oval Test) and I discovered that my figures were 6 for 20 (identical to Ray's on that sensational day, though well below his pace of course) I was delirious with joy – and remain so at the memory of it. This double coincidence simply could not have been fabricated. The bond was sealed. I was on my way. Like hell. But at least Jim Laker, when umpiring in a press game decades later, after I'd flung a few roundarmers down, murmured "Raymond?"

In the years that followed I saw Ray at dinners and in press-boxes and, later, at the Gabba ground, where we mused about the state of things, though he was not one to look back all that much. Then, in the members' bar, around 1990, he murmured that he had been diagnosed with diabetes. His doctor had imposed a strict limit of three beers a day. So was this his first Fourex then? No, it was his third. And play hadn't yet started.

To see him with wife Peggy (who was his reason for moving north) in their Brisbane florist shop was to be bemused by the

Peaceful flower-seller, with wife Peggy

sight of a man, once known as "Killer" and who petrified batsmen, now stacking bouquets of roses and chrysanthemums. The Queensland cricket fraternity staged a testimonial lunch for him, but when a Test batsman of later vintage hardly mentioned Ray in what was supposed to be the keynote speech, indignation drove me to ask the chairman if I might say a few words.

Given the chance, I made the point that the former Test record-holder was revered and cherished not only in his native land but in England too. Ray blushed.

As for that generous car ride so long ago, when the Lord's Taverners staged a memorable gala dinner in London for Compton, Edrich, Lindwall and Miller 30-odd years later, around midnight, when only the most committed bon viveurs remained, I asked Ray if transport back to his hotel had been arranged. It hadn't, so I said, "Come on, Ray, I'll give you a lift." It was a very gratifying moment.

Although never at ease speech-making, Ray Lindwall did his
bit at a memorable Taverners dinner in London

Arthur Mailey

1886-1967

That Worldly-Wise Grin

I WATCHED spellbound as Arthur Mailey spun his erratic magic on the giant silver screen, bobbing in to bowl to Sutcliffe at the MCG in the 1920s. Jack Gregory, between taking catches at short slip off his bowling, thundered in to unleash terror from the other end. To the audience at the recital of old newsreels in the vast chamber of Sydney Town Hall, Mailey was about twenty feet tall.

Soon afterwards this teenager discovered that Mailey was only the same height as himself. He was presenting caps to us one evening after we had won some colts competition. Inscrutable features, grey hair, a droll delivery and worldly-wise grin were unforgettable. When he demonstrated spinners' grips I noticed how strong his fingers seemed, the legacy of his days as a young glassblower, twiddling the glass flutes in furnace conditions. It helped strengthen his wrists too, and his lungs – though he claimed that his English mate, essayist Neville Cardus, was unimpressed by his appeals, which were little more than whimpers.

Of the entertaining anecdotes dutifully regaled by Arthur on that distant night, one stood out. He took 9 for 121 (still an Australian Test record) against England at Melbourne in the fourth Test of 1920-21, a series in which his then-supreme 36 wickets hurried Australia to their first 5-0 whitewash over England. Back home in Sydney, with the ball suitably decorated with an inscribed silver band, he awoke to discordant noises. His son was using the ball in a backyard game. The adornment was ruined. Typically, Arthur shrugged it off – or so he said.

Next season I got his autograph by the SCG pavilion and tried to engage him in conversation, but he was in a hurry. All the same, a lad who was trying to bat like Hutton

The droll Mailey pretends to be camera-shy

and bowl like Lindwall was bedazzled by the Mailey legend and lured towards the mystique of leg-spin. Arthur had dispensed it so enterprisingly that those

Mailey has Sutcliffe caught at slip by Gregory during the 1924-25 series.
The author gratefully reflects on acquaintance with all three

on the pitch could hear the ball buzzing. His length wasn't consistent, but who cared? He could bowl the unplayable. (He also employed resin on his fingers until scandalised.)

So that might have been that. But the bank transferred me to its Cronulla branch, down by the Pacific beachfront, and one of the local traders maintaining an account there was none other than Mr A.A.Mailey. I pleaded with the manager to introduce me, and every time Arthur came in I sidled over to launch a fresh barrage of questions. Modest and cautious replies came back. His memory wasn't all that good.

Mailey had enjoyed his trips to England as a player, journalist and cartoonist, but when it came to a question about his 10 for 66 against Gloucestershire during the Australians' 38-match 1921 tour, he simply grinned, shrugged and dismissed it as "my lucky day". I was probably given the standard jokes about his 4 for 362 in a Sheffield Shield match in 1926: just finding his length as Victoria's innings closed for 1107; chap in a brown top-coat dropped two catches off him in the pavilion enclosure.

Mailey's reputation locally was fairly ripe. On his shop window he had daubed an autobiographical trade plea: "I bowled tripe, I wrote tripe, now I sell it". They say he used to get away from the real world in his little boat, floating down Burraneer Bay, hoping the fish wouldn't bite too persistently.

Soon afterwards he wrote his life story. *10 for 66 and All That* was a landmark book, with some shrewd passages interspersed with much humour. It also has the reproduction of an oil he painted of the cricket ground at Royal Sandringham, a clue as to how far in society this man from the slums of Sydney had charmed his way.

He reckoned he was cleaning a water-meter under a coolabar tree when he discovered his selection for Australia for the first time. Delirious with joy, he began to worry years later if that old lady's water supply was ever reconnected.

I could have done with a lot more of Arthur Mailey's company.

Enjoying life was Mailey's principal aim, never better exemplified than on a long and leisurely voyage to England, as here in 1953 (photograph by Lindsay Hassett)

Peter May

1929-1994

He Never Wavered

IT WAS a classic case of false perception: Peter Barker Howard May (Charterhouse, Cambridge, Royal Navy, Surrey, England) had a choirboy appearance and was tall and square-shouldered, with a rather stiff gait, trim hair and a somewhat shy manner. However, as I came to realise, "PBH" was actually a man of steely determination and obstinacy. And he probably still ranks as England's finest batsman since 1939, Kevin Pietersen notwithstanding.

P.B.H.May: for some time the finest batsman in the world

A boyhood pledge was to name my first-born son after whoever happened to be the world's best batsman at that time. Thus, in 1958, our Peter was born. Friends have since teased about the choice of name: why wasn't he christened Garfield, or maybe Hanif? But Peter it was, and at the touring team's SCG net practice I had the gratification of informing the England captain, who had recently taken twin centuries off An Australian XI at Sydney and been chucked out by Jim Burke for 92 in the Test match. He did not seem moved by the news; but that hardly mattered at that euphoric time.

Across later decades, in social situations, I often reminded PBH of this nomenclature thing, but he never wavered: he was not embarrassed; simply uninterested. I grew to recognise that here was a pretty unsentimental fellow – in fact a hard man.

It's not that he lacked sensitivity. Harsh criticism of his "match-losing" duck on the final day of the dramatic Ashes Test at Old Trafford in 1961, coupled with serious health concerns and the urgency of making a living in the City (he had been, of course, an "unpaid" cricketer), had nudged him into premature and lamented retirement. He'd also earlier nursed resentment at the criticism when his fiancee Virginia joined him during the

1958-59 tour of Australia. Some reporters saw her presence as an unwarranted distraction; for others coarse envy showed in days when the professionals weren't well paid.

Years later May took charge of Test selection, and it was soon apparent that his word was absolute. Still boyish-looking in his fifties, he brooked no argument. When Micky Stewart was appointed as England's first-ever team coach, Peter was asked at a small luncheon gathering whether he thought it would work. "Micky," he said, in that silken and slightly nasal voice, "did as he was told as a player, and he'll do as he's told now." There was the faintest semblance of that familiar angled grin. Despite his mild and conservative appearance he could have been a latterday D.R.Jardine.

Oops! May's stump is broken by West Indies tearaway Wes Hall

Around this time, I pleaded on behalf of a young television reporter for PBH to recant and give him a few words. I might as well have asked Mother Teresa to blaspheme. This was the man who had stood up to the formidable F.R.Brown, manager on that contentious 1958-59 Ashes tour. It would not have been often that he changed his mind over anything.

One winter evening around 1979 I found myself speaking alongside him at a village club supper. A questioner asked about the likely impact of the Packer intervention, which had shaken us all. I was trying to identify some benefits which might serve as some comfort, such as more money for top players. Peter May swiftly broke in: "I think we've had enough on this subject!" Yes, captain.

Our final conversation was on a balcony at Lord's, and with his health in decline and his finances precariously placed, he described his situation as being like staring into an abyss. I considered reminding him one more time that I'd named that baby after him, but decided against.

It was not the man in the grey suit I want to remember. It was the fresh-faced young Englishman who swung the Sydney Test match of December 1954. His century stand with young Colin Cowdrey set it up for "Typhoon" Tyson to storm in and blow Australia away. A PBH four pulled to midwicket off Archer is preserved among the most precious visuals in my mind. And next morning, 98 overnight, he drove Lindwall square for four, reaching a hundred that was to propel England to a famous comeback victory and turn a series.

Four years later I was ready with a camera as he drove Benaud to the pickets, reaching yet another SCG century in the NSW match. Thank God for film.

Sydney Cricket Ground 1958-59: having been 99 not out since Saturday evening, after the rest day Peter May resumes on the Monday and drives the first ball, from Richie Benaud, to the pickets in front of the old Brewongle Stand. A treasured picture, previously unpublished, from the author's new camera

Ernie McCormick
1906-1991
Terrorised The Don

SOME ARE remembered for the wrong reasons. Ernie McCormick was Australia's outstanding fast bowler of the 1930s, yet many people remember him as just the poor wretch who began the 1938 tour of England with a ridiculous series of no-balls at Worcester in the opening match. (Umpires' tolerance and laxness in all the years of the back-foot no-ball law, together with the undue advantage gained by wide-striding fast bowlers who dragged, forced the switch to the front-foot clause about 30 years later.)

That spring day in 1938 poor Ernie was simply incapable of adjusting his landing point. Umpire Harry Baldwin called him eight times in his first over and nine times in his second, during which the opener Charlie Bull had his eyebrow cut in attempting a hook. McCormick was called for 35 no-balls in that match and forever afterwards made people laugh by claiming that it might have been even worse, only the umpire – to whom he apologised for causing so much trouble – became hoarse, then lost his voice completely.

Another of his little jokes was to feign deafness when anyone raised the subject. Quietly he held the view that English umpires had it in for him after Bradman had claimed upon arriving in England that he was the fastest bowler

A memorable over: McCormick at Worcester bowling no-ball after no-ball

163

in the world.

The high spot for Ernie on that 1938 tour was the Lord's Test, when he tore through England's top order – Hutton, Barnett and Edrich – only for Hammond to play perhaps his greatest innings. It ended: b McCormick 240. Although his tour was not all that successful, controversy surrounded his omission from the Oval Test on supposed fitness grounds. England could surely not have reached 903 for 7 had he taken the new ball instead of the gentle Waite and McCabe.

McCormick had done well in his first Test series, in South Africa in 1935-36, and at the Gabba in December 1936 he became only the second* Australian to take a wicket with his first ball in an Ashes Test (Arthur Coningham was the first and only Shane Warne has joined the list since). In the Grimmett-O'Reilly era of spin domination Ernie supplied the hot pace at the start. So hostile

The joker and his wife: Ernie and Kathleen McCormick

could he be that even Don Bradman was thought to be reluctant to face him in one particular state match. When Ernie finished that 1936-37 season with 9 for 40 at Adelaide, in the match that secured the Shield for Victoria, The Don (8) was one of his victims.

* It has since been discovered that Tom Horan also did so (at Sydney in January 1883).

Despite the hostility he was one of the funniest of cricketers. He never tired of telling everybody about the chap at the 1977 Centenary Test who came up and said: "Hey, didn't you used to be Ernie McCormick?" Spending a day with him and wife Kathleen at their Queensland Gold Coast home was a tonic. Chuckles and belly laughs punctuated the stories.

He had been taught well: the legendary Ted McDonald, master of rhythm and high pace, coached him after he had abandoned wicketkeeping in favour of fast bowling ("I laid my club captain out in the nets.").

As a confirmed No.10 or 11 he said it was a good spot as you always had company when you left the field.

Ever the joker, McCormick in costume, England 1938

Once he and his mates were misunderstood: when Jack Badcock bagged a pair in the 1938 Lord's Test, sympathetic Ernie urged the players to say nothing when the batsman returned. It backfired. "A bloke makes a pair," Badcock whined. "You wouldn't think your mates would give you the arse too!"

Ernie had recently had a visit from two of his pre-war team-mates, Bill Brown and Len Darling. The recollection triggered another bout of laughter: "We were all telling lies!"

A jeweller/instrument-maker by profession, McCormick had been commissioned to make the Frank Worrell Trophy, and was amused to have a repeat request years later after the West Indies Board managed to lose it. Then the original was found.

In 1977 he made the trophy awarded to Dennis Lillee after the Centenary Test. There can have been nothing to choose between those two tearaways in their prime with a new ball in their hungry fingers.

Colin Milburn
1941-1990
He Lifted All Around Him

IF THERE was one player the game could least afford to lose in the late 1960s it was roly-poly Colin Milburn, the chuckling heavyweight from Northants via County Durham. In a manner of speaking (pure Geordie in his case) he defied his unathletic physique, batting for England with thrilling aggression and a technique that was more textbook than many observers understood. Bare-headed, shirt buttons undone, sleeves rolled to the biceps, sweat splashing

Among the most breathtaking spectacles of the 1960s was the Milburn pull shot

from his chubby, pink face, he lifted souls as he lofted sixes.

From his brave Test debut 94 at Old Trafford against West Indies in 1966, followed by an unbeaten 126 in the Lord's Test, to Brisbane, where he belted an incredible 243 for Western Australia in a Shield match, he left some colossal marks. Only a few weeks before the horrible road accident that ended it all in 1969, "Ollie" had made a disciplined 139 at the National Stadium, Karachi in a Test match which was abandoned on the third day after rioting. It was the last of Milburn's 16 innings for England.

Nine Tests, average 46.71. And that was it. He was 28. The selectors should have backed him more often. He may not have been an outfielder but he was a fine, brave short leg before unfair fielding helmets came in. How Ollie would have relished Twenty20. And how Twenty20 crowds would have loved him.

Following the violent, messy car crash in Northampton which cost him his left eye, he amazed everyone by assuring them that he was determined to play again at top level. But in 1973, in 16 matches, he averaged only 19. In 1974 this slipped to 12. Only once in those 43 innings did he manage a fifty. That was against Surrey at Guildford, late August 1973. After a first-innings duck, in the follow-on Milburn withstood the seam and swerve of Geoff Arnold and Robin Jackman, even sweeping the latter for six into the groundsman's garden. From the sadness emerged a glimmer of hope as he worked his way to 57. Then Intikhab bowled him around his stubby legs. Milburn's solitary eye and those chunky forearms had done their work. Optimism was revived.

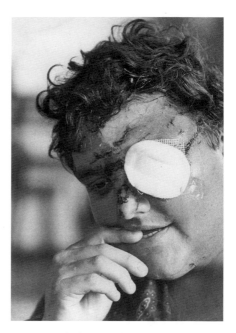

Tragedy has struck: Colin Milburn about to leave hospital

We chatted afterwards and he talked of his dream of making it back into the Western Australia side next winter (he failed to do so). He confessed that he was hopeless with money and left it to others to supervise his benefit pool and modest savings. Leaving the testimonial proceeds in his hands would have been "chaotic". Another thing he had in common with Victor Trumper was that he was restless behind a shop counter, so that had to end.

He had done some television commentary and was good at it, because he spoke his mind and had a pleasing voice and dared to enjoy a laugh. More of that perhaps? No, the BBC didn't seem to want him. He was currently engaged to a lass. (That too was not to be.) This lovable man was drawing too many short straws.

In the years left to him (he was only 48 when he died) Milburn could not stay away from his beloved game, or more specifically the broad companionship that surrounds it. He drank a lot. We heard his roars of laughter even before spotting him in hotel bars. Many a night he finished up on a pal's settee, or even on the floor. Knowing his love of powerful music, as I drove him back from a match one evening I put a Jethro Tull tape on with a special drum turn, the volume high. The car throbbed. I thought I saw his foot tapping, though

The batsman clown deep in reflection aboard the Jolly Roger in Bridgetown Harbour

there was no vocalising. When the number finished I asked him what he thought. "'Sorl rait," he murmured. For the first and only time I felt slight disappointment with this hero of the people.

He came to the Caribbean with us on a group tour, and diminished the local rum supplies significantly. He performed his duties full-heartedly, splashing about in the sea and chatting and laughing with the paying tourists, who, without exception, loved him.

But there was one haunting moment when I looked across the deck of the booze-cruise vessel *Jolly Roger* and saw Ollie suddenly alone, flopped on a hatchway, plastic tumbler in hand, absurd pirate's hat on his head, one eye artificial, the other one gazing vacantly. This supremely companionable fellow looked so forlorn. This vision, seen beside a mental film clip of his fearless hooking of Hall and Griffith, was an unbearably poignant image of a stirring character.

Keith Miller
1919-2004
Keep Something in Reserve

AS WITH so many friendships, it began with an autograph. Evenings by the SCG pavilion doors were tense with expectation, and never was there such an exit as Keith Miller's. Resplendent dark hair swept back, smart double-breasted suit, radiant smile: here was cricket's Gary Cooper, without the diffidence. All the lads were keen to speak to him, apart from a few who were overawed and tongue-tied. He never let us down. And the most extraordinary thing was his novel way of signing: "eith iller" – then the flamboyant insertion of the K and the M. It was probably his way of dealing with the boredom of repetition.

Just over sixty years ago he scored a century at the SCG on my baptism as a Test spectator. Much later, whenever I harked back to that he claimed to have no recall of it. Cricket was just one part of his life, not the be-all and end-all. As time passed, increased media attention was devoted to his war service as a Mosquito pilot, and the truth was that *this* was perceived to be the highlight of his life. He even nursed some bitterness: "I think I won a few Sheffield Shields for 'em [NSW], but there's not even a bit of graffiti here [the SCG] in my name."

Much-feared bowler

IIe enjoyed life to the full, "relating" to the ordinary folk and the female of the species and the famous (especially war heroes such as Douglas Bader and Hughie Edwards VC). To walk round the ground with him was to be on a meet-the-people exercise. At Lord's, where his bold batting and hurricane fast bowling had been as dramatically displayed as at the SCG, he would halt every few paces to chat to friends and strangers. At Hove, resplendent in herringbone sports jacket, he strolled around as if it were a Paris catwalk. John Arlott was with us, and the cricket was ignored as people called out or simply stared agog at the glamorous pair of celebrities. "Nugget" loved it.

It was probably not just the war experience with its exhilaration and tragic undertones that rendered Miller such an affable man. At school in Melbourne he was small, teased and unsuccessful. So even when he'd turned into a superb athlete and then a feted airman, he still intuitively went on craving affection and approval. This was evident in his gregariousness. Not that he didn't make enemies. Authority didn't trust him, so he never captained Australia. As with Shane Warne, it was a golden opportunity missed.

Keith Miller knew as well as any man how to relax: photo by John Woodcock

In 1986 Keith showed up unexpectedly at the A.E.Stoddart 485 centenary match at Hampstead – where a ladyfriend happened to live. Great to see him, but what was he doing here? He mumbled about wanting to be part of an historic occasion. At a Lord's Taverners banquet he brought his diminutive mate Scobie Breasley along and spent all evening introducing the champion jockey to everyone he bumped into.

On the morning of a Test in the late 1980s, it was chilling to see him sinking onto a low wall in St John's Wood Road after a dizzy spell. It was like witnessing a special boxer's first collapse.

He loved to dispense his little pearls of wisdom. "Can you remember what you were worrying about a year ago?" Well, actually, I could. So he passed on that one. But something else he said was later to come in very useful: "Remember: always keep something in reserve. Hold something back."

In 1993 I sat with him in the studio where the finishing touches were being applied to the controversial portrait commissioned by MCC. I had a tape recorder and hoped to do a comprehensive interview. But, as always, cricket facts and figures meant nothing. He wanted to talk only about the war. The loss of some mates during a German bombing raid on Bournemouth while he was away playing cricket tortured him, irrationally but darkly. It's known as survivor's guilt.

I choked at the sight of the most glamorous cricketer of the 20th century struggling to get into the car, his sticks getting tangled, the odd oath flying. I dropped him off at the home of a couple of WAAF friends from the war years. Those adoring ladies called him "Dusty" and spoke of the nights he'd flown off into the sinister distance, leaving them wondering if they'd ever see him again.

Flamboyant batsman

Leo O'Brien
1907-1997
"Hey, I'm the Left-hander!"

THERE WERE very few laughs to be had during the ill-tempered Bodyline season of 1932-33 but Leo O'Brien, the little Aussie left-hander, passed on a couple. When five Englishmen formed a close-packed leg-side field as Bill Woodfull took strike, Leo, wide-eyed and innocent, said, "Hey, it's the right-hander down that end. I'm the left-hander!" The Poms just smiled and Harold Larwood set about pummelling the ribs of the Australian XI batsmen.

O'Brien, like the rest, wore a cap and was protected by only a box, with an old singlet tucked down his thigh and those sad rubber-nipple gloves, one of which he gave me for my little museum. He was going to hand over his old bat too until he found that it was ravaged by woodworm.

"There wasn't much you could duck. It came at your throat, really fast!"

Game for anything: Leo O'Brien cracks a pull shot

Interestingly he picked out his fellow Victoria leftie Len Darling: "He used to stand up and hook Larwood square."

Leo ("Mo" to his many mates) top-scored with 46 in two-and-a-half hours in that pre-Test encounter at the MCG, when Don Bradman (36 in 46 minutes) "was like a cat on hot bricks" as Larwood, Bowes and Voce bounced him. Yet, but for a doubtful lbw against him that a modern referral would probably have overturned, had Bradman's frenzied counter-attack continued it might just have persuaded the England camp that "fast leg theory" was not the answer, thus depriving history of its most sensational interlude.

Leo was always the first person I sought out in Melbourne in the 1970s and 1980s. We encamped at the bar and between sips he would talk about boxing (he won all his lightweight bouts except the last), his baseball and Aussie Rules football, his horse-training and, most of all, his beloved cricket. With the set hair-parting and slow drawl of that special breed, the friendly pre-war Aussie bloke, he loved recalling the cricketers of the

Full of beans (and anecdotes) when the sporting days were past

1930s. Three or four anecdotes per beer materialised, one of them revealing that he was one of the few opponents the haughty England captain Jardine bothered to address.

On his Test debut, in the second Test of 1932-33 (which was to remain Australia's only victory in the series), Leo was sent in ahead of Bradman, who was surprised when he saw the left-hander padding up. Bill Woodfull had pinned up the order, and there it was: Woodfull, Fingleton, O'Brien, Bradman .... Leo was run out for 10 (65 minutes) after a risky call by Fingleton and was still ruminatively unbuckling his pads when The Don came back, out first ball. "He said he'd been bowled. Didn't mention that he'd played on to Bowes. Very modest bloke."

In the second innings Larwood sent O'Brien's off stump flying for 11 and

O'Brien the young all-round sportsman

that was that – until he was recalled for the fifth Test, when he made a brave if lucky 61 at Sydney.

In the meantime he had been twelfth man in the stormy Adelaide Test, when Woodfull's stinging private censure of the hand-wringing England manager Plum Warner was sensationally leaked to a newspaper. For years the question raged: who told the reporter? Leo, a witness to the famous exchange, said he knew. Then he said he would tell me some other time.

I could hardly wait for our next session. He slowly lit his pipe, then, by a process of elimination, he got to the point. In that room with Woodfull, he said, had been Alan Kippax (who was not playing), former players Jack Ryder and Ernie Jones, and a physio who was "stone deaf". So? But he remained evasive, although he did confirm that, with all the Australian players sitting just outside the Adelaide dressing-room, the story spread quickly: and it was Leo who had told them. But which of them, if any, told the pressman?

Publication of Leo's teasing response sparked a stampede of interviews. To my surprise he gave varying accounts to others. When I wrote to him, he dealt elegantly with the situation: "I have soon adjusted their ideas to some order."

Years after he died I was able to uncover the name of the cricketer who did leak the incident. Whether Leo really knew all along that it was not Fingleton but almost certainly Bradman, I shall never know.

Bert Oldfield

1894-1976

Gentleman Wicketkeeper

BERT OLDFIELD'S sports shop in Sydney was an Aladdin's cave for a starry-eyed boy in the 1950s. There in the Hunter Street shop window was the dramatic life-size cut-out of Wally Hammond's cover-drive (Oldfield crouched low behind the stumps). Near the entrance was another: Tibby Cotter full-length, the speed terror from Mr Oldfield's own club, Glebe. Tibby was killed at Beersheba in 1917 while serving with the AIF. Bert Oldfield came close that same year when a shell-burst killed the other three stretcher bearers and their wounded soldier during the fierce fighting at Polygon Wood. He was dug from the thick mud and gore, convalesced in Gloucester and was in love with England thereafter.

He once indicated where the metal plate had been inserted into his skull, the same smiling head that a Larwood bouncer clanged during the Bodyline Tests of 1932-33. Bert Oldfield was a survivor.

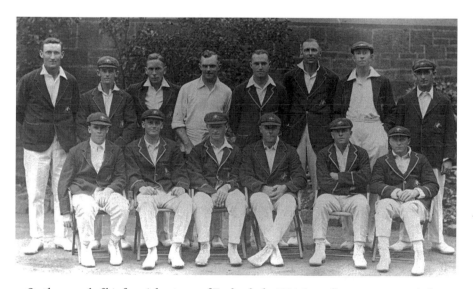

On the second of his four Ashes tours of England: the 1926 Australian team: rear – Arthur Richardson, Johnny Taylor, Arthur Mailey, Jack Ellis, Sam Everett, Jack Gregory, Jack Ryder, Tommy Andrews; seated – Bill Ponsford, Bill Woodfull, Clarrie Grimmett, Warren Bardsley (acting captain), Charlie Macartney, Bert Oldfield. Missing are skipper Herbie Collins, who was enduring a bout of neuritis, and Hunter Hendry, who missed much of the tour through scarlet fever

175

He was also a gentle, fastidious, courteous man, qualities not uncommon in Australians of earlier generations. Always immaculately dressed, he favoured a waistcoat and starched shirt-collar. His voice was crisp, diction precise. Renowned as a gentleman wicketkeeper, he played in 38 Ashes Tests between the world wars, and once held the Test dismissals record: 130 including 52 stumpings. They say he sent his victims on their way almost with an apology.

I bought my first bat from him for £2 and he added a free tin of bat oil. On another momentous occasion he presented me with his 1930 Australian Test blazer and a ball from the Trent Bridge Test of that summer, igniting my mania for cricket memorabilia. In 1954 he raised a team to play against the Pakistan High Commissioner's XI. At sixty he still moved with ease behind the stumps, an elegance that stopped just short of showiness.

One day I scratched a lift with him to the Sydney Cricket Ground. He spoke with pride at having scored a century in every country he had toured, and that included Ethiopia. With painful reluctance I had to exit the car at

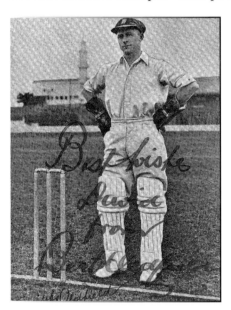

Bert Oldfield, gentleman wicketkeeper

the members' gate. Still, I could always go back to the shop and lap up further musings covering the halcyon days of England v Australia Test cricket. He spoke fondly of Jack Hobbs and Herbert Sutcliffe, of Maurice Tate and Arthur Gilligan, and of the hospitality he had enjoyed all over the British Isles during the 1919 Australian Imperial Forces tour, four Ashes tours and several more visits as a commentator.

Clem was the senior assistant in the shop, and it was he who, in 1926, had raced some proper equipment out to the SCG for the ill-clad youngster who had just come up from the bush for trials: D.G.Bradman. Don never liked that tale, and denied it. Furthermore, Bertie had run him out as he was leading Australia's victory surge in the Adelaide Test in 1928-29 (England won by 12 runs.) The impression was that they were never bosom pals.

*Hospitable hosts: Mr and Mrs Bert Oldfield in 1972, with the
author's wife (right) and two sons*

There was a lapse of ten years before I saw Bert Oldfield again on my return
to Sydney in 1971. We visited him at his home in Killara – the cricket oval there
now bears his name. He gave my sons a signed bat. Later I was entertained
to lunch in town at the Imperial Services Club: another magic carpet ride with
a catalogue of visions from another age and its fascinating cricketers. As we
left mid-afternoon, Mr Oldfield linked his arm through mine as we crossed
George Street. Chaps used to do this unabashed in the 1920s and 1930s.

Cars are driven even more madly in Sydney than in London, and suddenly
a Holden was roaring straight at us. I leapt for the kerb, dragging the little
wicketkeeper with me. What the Kaiser's army and Jardine's bouncer brigade
failed to do no lousy driver was going to succeed in doing.

This precious little gentleman was to live a further five years. As with all
these veterans, the wish is that they could have lived forever.

Norman O'Neill
1937-2008
A Precious Life Saved

LATE 1952, and what were regarded as the pick of the colts from Sydney's St George area are gathering for the opening match of the A.W.Green Shield Under-16 inter-club tournament. One of our number, Reg Gasnier, is destined to become one of Australia's finest-ever Rugby League footballers. Another, Norman O'Neill, is soon to be tagged "the new Bradman" – poor fella.

With his Mr Universe build and Hollywood looks, the abundantly talented Norm was made captain. He stroked heaps of runs and garnered wickets with his leg-spinners and wrong'uns, and equally spectacularly he'd split stumps with his rocket returns from cover point. Backed by the disciplinarian seniors in a club for which Bradman, O'Reilly, Lindwall and Morris had all played, O'Neill read the game as smartly as a veteran.

Batting with Norm was both inspiring and intimidating. Dreamy youth, I wanted to be not only the next Len Hutton but Ray Lindwall too. Norm gave me the new ball, and I did my best with it. One evening, when we were battling for a draw, he called out, "Dave, do your bootlace up!" I looked down. The laces were fine. I shrugged. He repeated what in reality was a command. Ah, I got it. I was to slow down the action, play for time, ignore the umpire. (No minimum number of overs in those days.) I fiddled with my laces while the batsmen and umpires seethed.

I took a catch, and my captain's iron handshake numbed my fingers. Our third-wicket partnership was rather one-sided. He crunched anything short through a helpless cover field. Only Gordon Greenidge and Robin Smith have cut so powerfully since. Meanwhile I swished away, mainly in vain. We put on 44, my contribution 10. That night I told my father that I'd been batting with a Test batsman of the future.

It must be noted, however, that there may never have been an N.C.L.O'Neill (2779 runs at 45.55 in 42 Tests) had I not lurched across and grabbed his arm when he lost his grip on a slippery support bar and staggered as our speeding open-doored train lurched towards Hurstville for a Green Shield match one hot and sticky morning. Something, probably a girl on the footpath way below us, had deflected his attention and, stepping towards the gap, he came within a whisker of tumbling to his death. It was natural to reflect on this in subsequent summers as I watched him cracking runs for New South Wales and Australia.

Memory's other 1952-53 cameos are few but precious: another of those Tarzan handshakes after batting out for a draw at Waverley; half-suppressed hilarity all over the field as our captain's leg-breaks were smashed all around Bankstown Oval by a tiny mop-haired kid; concern when one of Norm's cannonball throws burst through keeper Laurie Kennedy's gloves, thudding into his chest and causing him to spit blood for the rest of the day; and collective

The exciting duel continues: Fred Trueman v Norman O'Neill

despair when we found we'd missed out on the Shield by a decimal point.

Norm was soon in the big time, scoring a rare thousand first-class runs in 1957-58, then, a year later, illuminating his first Ashes Test match with a brilliant 71 not out to steer Australia to victory in an otherwise morbid event. There was, naturally, always a special personal feel when watching him bat, and endless admiration for his beautiful strokeplay: the decisive late cut, the savage pull, and most impressive of all, the drive off the back foot, when his left elbow was so high in the perpendicular as to seem an anatomical impossibility. This stroke brought him several straight fours off West Indies thunderbolt Wes Hall in the Brisbane tied Test of 1960, when O'Neill scored 181.

I saw little of him in later years. There was coffee in Norm's motel room during the 1977 Centenary Test in Melbourne, and occasional chats at the bar. When his son Mark played in a match at Eastbourne, when I went out to umpire I pleaded with him not to get his pads in front as it would break my sentimental heart to give Norm's son out.

Norm and I last spoke one evening in Johannesburg in 1989, when he and others, including Denis Compton and Mike Procter, were discussing how a mixed-race South African tour of Australia might be organised. Norm insisted that he and his wife Gwen could take care of the players' laundry.

A few years later I spotted him in the broadcasting area at the Gabba. I needed to ask somebody who it was, so ravaged by his final illness was my former St George pride and inspiration.

Australia's pin-up boy of the late 1950s, Norm O'Neill
(John Woodcock)

Bill O'Reilly
1905-1992
Rarely a Tear

"IF EVER you see a coach coming, run for your life." And Bill O'Reilly was not referring to a bus. "Tiger" believed in playing cricket as comes naturally. And what a player he was. Tall, bald and ugly, he bowled brisk, bouncy leg-spin variations and snarled a lot. In 19 Ashes Tests from Bodyline to 1938 he disposed of 102 Englishmen. And if it was suggested that the Yorkshire left-hander Maurice Leyland often had the better of him, he would bounce straight back: "And how many times did I get him out?" It was nine, in 16 Tests, albeit with decreasing frequency, though you dared not put it like that. He troubled them all, including England's greatest, Hammond, Sutcliffe and Hendren.

Bill simply thrived on confrontation. I sat with him through many a Test match and relished his strong opinions. He hated one-day cricket. He thought it should be called Crack-it, and refused to write about it.

"There's Britain up to her old colonial tricks again," whined this very Irish Australian after the Falklands War. I wasn't going to stand for that, and after words were exchanged he chose not to speak to me during the second and third days' play. What, I asked, would Australia do if some foreign force occupied Lord Howe Island?

Then it was all right again, and I was relieved because it was a privilege to know the man generally regarded as the world's best-ever bowler, perhaps on a par with S.F.Barnes.

I'd played for O'Reilly's great club, St George, which influenced him to write a foreword to my book on

William Joseph "Tiger" O'Reilly, perhaps the best bowler of all time?

the 1978-79 Ashes series. His essay was so generous that I wonder if he was perhaps taking the mick a little? But there was a kindliness about him, even if another no-go area was Don Bradman, his old Test colleague and captain, for whom he had little time. He knew of Don's friendship with that lively little left-hander Jock Livingston – later of Northants, he had made his New South

O'Reilly, the purveyor of fastish leg-spin variations, with hostile accompaniment

Wales debut a week before Pearl Harbor, keeping wicket to O'Reilly – and as Jock and I climbed the steps of the M.A.Noble Stand one morning, Tiger bellowed: "Been to Bowral lately?" Heads turned.

Bill's dedication to spin showed in a devout backing for the young leggie Kerry O'Keeffe, which touched embarrassing heights. I was present when another promising colt, Adrian Tucker, was introduced to the great man. Bill was fatherly towards him and, of course, right on the ball: "Show me your field placing for the wrong'un," he croaked. He hummed approvingly when Adrian marked out his field setting on the notepad.

Indulgence had its limits though. When Geoff Lawson wrote to him complaining about some harsh comments in the *Sydney Morning Herald*, former schoolmaster O'Reilly returned the latter splattered with green-ink corrections to the syntax.

In the late 1950s there was a joint testimonial for Bill and his old mate Stan McCabe. To see the McCabe swivel hook and the huffing, puffing, bent-kneed O'Reilly in action at North Sydney Oval was to be transported back to the 1930s. The one was as reticent as the other was outgoing. Years later, asked where McCabe's shots went during that famous 187 against Bodyline here at the Sydney Cricket Ground, Bill jabbed a forefinger: "There! And there! And there! And there!" You could visualise the ball bouncing back off those lovely old white pickets leg-side both ends.

Bill's last days were wretched. Part of a leg had been amputated and, when I rang him with a view to popping in, since I was passing through Blakehurst, he declined, saying he was busy nowadays staring at the kitchen wall to make sure nobody ran off with it. My mistake might have been to mention that I had Jock Livingston with me.

His final match as a correspondent had been the Bicentennial Test at the SCG in 1988, when he was 82, and from the adjacent seat I watched in wonder as one pilgrim after another came to pay homage and to get his signature. Finally the cricket writers presented him with a weighty book of mine, *Pageant of Cricket*, and at long last we had visible evidence that this big, bluff man was as vulnerable as the rest of us: a tear or two showed at the corners of those rheumy old eyes.

Kerry Packer
1937-2005
The Man Who Remoulded the Game

HE WAS the man who upended the cricket world with an audacious venture, a series of international matches for his own television channel. Inevitably he split that world into two camps. Much ill-feeling and lashings of money was spilt before an awkward peace eventually came, spurred by the victory he had secured in the High Court in London. Those who had wished to see media mogul Kerry Packer sent packing were grievously disappointed.

Opinions might have been less inflammatory had this Australian heavyweight with flattened features and a steady flow of aggressive utterances instead been someone diminutive and whimsical such as, say, Lindsay Hassett or Ronnie Corbett, less overtly menacing. Yet those close to Packer worshipped him (allowing that cricketers and others on his payroll needed very large bags to accommodate their earnings).

During the High Court hearing I was struck by Packer's calm poise and

Kerry Packer shows he can play a bit too: in the slips line-up with David Frith and Ian Chappell, Harrogate, Yorkshire, 1977 (Patrick Eagar photograph)

politeness in the witness stand. "His" cricketers had testified in a variety of ways: Alan Knott whiningly, John Snow peremptorily, Mike Procter with limbs in a tangle as he tried desperately to look relaxed.

Suddenly, Kerry Packer was going to play in our "Ashes Press Test" at Harrogate. I didn't believe Ian Chappell at first, but sure enough the biggest 1977 celebrity in the wide world of cricket kitted himself out at Harrods and arrived in Yorkshire by helicopter. Surrounded by cream-clad media men, Packer played it cool. He was there not to give press conferences but to enjoy the game. Ian Wooldridge cleverly lured him from the hurlyburly, offering him a loosening hit-up on the tennis court. An exclusive *Daily Mail* interview resulted.

Kerry was friendly to all in the confines of the changing-room, quickly dispersing any trepidation – until he reached for his boots. I'd never seen such massive and somehow intimidating feet as he plonked them up on the table. Soon we (I was in the Australian Press XI this time) were batting. The runs piled up until, with three overs left, my partner and I agreed that the small crowd of noisy Yorkshiremen had come to see not us but K.F.B.Packer. So I ran my partner out.

And in came the big man, the name on the lips of everyone in world cricket. He patted his first ball to cover and seemed uncertain whether to try for an impossible run. In the spirit of the occasion I gave him, just for fun, the old Compton call of "Yes! No! Wait!!" Packer frowned. Over was called. He strode down the pitch. Was this giant going to wrap the bat around my skull for teasing him?

"Look," he breathed. "About the running."

"Yes?"

"I'm in your hands."

Kerry Packer *in my hands*? He said that. I swear he did. What would the cricket establishment have given to have had him say such a thing to them?

Well, after we'd fielded, with idle chatter between overs, we didn't meet again until the 1978-79 season, when the Ashes Tests clashed with the second of his World Series programmes. It was haunting to be at VFL Park for his "SuperTest", with hardly anyone in attendance despite the star players. Kerry's former social teammates were invited to the VIP area. There was beer and desultory, polite chat. I spotted on the giant TV screen that Gary Gilmour was spelt "Gilmore". I never could stand mis-spellings so I took the risk of drawing the big man's attention to it. "Have you got nothing better to do than nitpick?" he might have said. But he didn't. He whispered into a technician's ear and the matter was swiftly remedied. I was impressed.

Our paths crossed occasionally thereafter, and he reverted to the public perception of him: a heavyweight ever ready to land one on an adversary (for that is how I among many now appeared). Looking at my overnight bag with its Australian Cricket Board sponsor's logo, he sneered. I looked at him quizzically. What next? Was he about to bounce me for that misfired joke at Harrogate? "That bag," he roared, "won't last out the summer!"

Well, it did. And it's been housed in my library/museum to this day, a reminder of my encounters with the man who turned cricket into a garish branch of showbusiness.

*Back to business: the tycoon
continues his manoeuvres against the
cricket establishment*

Eddie Paynter
1901-1979
Heroism from a Hospital Bed

WITH THOSE mournful features and alert eyes he could have been one of those little Lancashire comedians from the music halls and films of his time. He even came from a place with an amusing name: Oswaldtwisle, where he was born in 1901, aptly on Guy Fawkes Day.

Eddie Paynter should have played many more Test matches. But for failure in the last of his 20, he would have averaged an awesome 63.79. As it was, against Australia he registered a colossal 84.42. He left some very notable feats behind him. The most renowned was his 83 at Brisbane during the Bodyline series of 1932-33, when he dragged his aching body from a hospital bed and saved England.

Wide-brimmed sunhat making the little fella look like a walking white mushroom, he batted through a decisive session as Australia pressed hard to level the series. It was said that the pills could be heard rattling in the bottle in his pocket as he scuttled singles. Three days later he whacked a six to bring

A run for Paynter during his famous innings in adversity at the Gabba during the Bodyline Test series

England a six-wicket victory and the Ashes. In 1990 someone sold that ball at auction for £4000. Paynter himself was short of funds right up to his death in 1979.

He could be spotted among the masses of old Test players in the guests'

enclosure at the MCG during that phenomenal 1977 Centenary Test match, when – the smallest figure in that crowded bar – he tried to get a beer amid the ceaseless clatter and nostalgia-fuelled chatter. It became ribald legend that Eddie was pleading for "a warm beer, please!"

He would not have been there but for funding raised at a special gala dinner. Yet here was a man who had scored two centuries and two double-centuries for his country, plus a 99 at Lord's in 1938: lbw to O'Reilly. Tiger Smith was the umpire who gave him out. Eddie was still slightly disgruntled when I visited him in Idle, Yorkshire, almost 40 years after that incident. "I hit it!" he exclaimed. Newsreel film shows him walking smartly away without dissent. His stand of 222 with the majestic Hammond (240) had saved England. Later in the match he kept wicket when Ames broke a finger.

Paynter, the prolific little Lancashire left-hander, indulges his favourite pull shot

Eddie was reclining on the carpet, and his son and grandson were there. (Years later, David, a great-grandson he never knew, showed promise with Northants, but it was not to be.) There was much to relive from the simple perspective of that living-room: Eddie's 322 at Hove in 1937, which came after an all-night train journey from the Manchester Test. Afterwards the Lancashire lads went ice-skating in Brighton and Paynter brought the house down with an impromptu pirouette.

The Test double-hundreds mesmerised me. I'd had a glimpse of some film of his effort in the first of the two Durban Tests of 1938-39. The commanding Hammond pounded drives through the off side, and there was Paynter, the sprightly tich, airborne to get on top of the ball, clipping it through the leg side with all sorts of inventive shots. In less than two hours they put on 242 for the third wicket, Eddie finishing with 243 –

having made twin centuries in the first Test.

It was another great distinction, for nobody had scored double-centuries for England against both Australia and South Africa. Only seven months earlier he had made his unbeaten 216 at Trent Bridge, briefly the highest by anyone against Australia in England. He cracked a smile at the thought of it. Yet this marvellous knock was overshadowed by Charlie Barnett's 98 before lunch, Ashes debut centuries by young Hutton and Compton, and then McCabe's truly glorious 232 which helped Australia to a draw in that four-day Test.

Eddie Paynter: desperate quest for warm beer in Melbourne

There is much film of this Test, though it was of slight comfort to this popular man who had struggled financially. Still, Eddie drew upon his reserves of pride and cheer, pointing out with a grin that he had topped the English bowling on that stormy 1932-33 tour of Australia. When asked to jot down his memories of that famous Brisbane Test, he recalled the obstructive hospital sister, who would take no responsibility for his absconding. But "after the match was over, I was smashing".

Ian Peebles

1908-1980

Gentleman Who Tested The Don

IAN PEEBLES was one of the few bowlers who confused Don Bradman. It was his rolling leg-spin variations, delivered with a high arm, which stopped – if only for one Test match – the mighty little Australian during his historic destructive trail through England in 1930. When it seemed that his 131, 254 and 334 in the first three Tests were pointing inevitably to a 400 in the next, at Old Trafford, on came the tall Scots-born Oxford University and Middlesex bowler to spin one through him first ball. He then had him dropped by Hammond. Finally, Duleepsinhji held a catch at second slip. The Don had scratched 14 and suddenly seemed mortal. For that brief period Peebles had toyed with him.

Having confounded most of the Australians, Peebles held his place for the final Test, and his heroic figures on that Oval featherbed were 6 for 204 off 71 overs. It had been a summer of productive toil: 13 wickets in the University match and also against Worcestershire, Hobbs and Sutcliffe among his 133 (18.44) for the season. No wonder his shoulder gave him pain, interrupting his career. Having begun as a fast-medium bowler before Aubrey Faulkner's

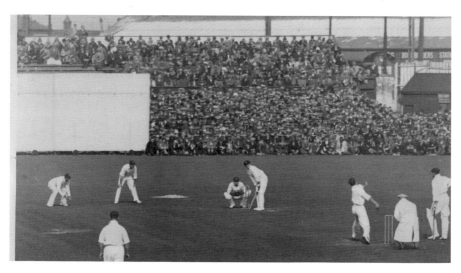

Ian Peebles bowls to Kippax in the 1930 Old Trafford Test, having had Bradman caught at slip for 14. It was the only Test of the series in which Bradman failed to make a century (or a double or triple)

encouragement to persevere with the brisk and amazing leg-spin variations, he was to have a vacillating career. But now here he was, at 23, a *Wisden* Cricketer of the Year.

Peebles had played the first of his 13 Test matches two years earlier in South Africa. There, during a minor match at Constantia, his non-presence was immortalised. The scorebook entry showed "absent, bathing 0". A carefree amateur was he, one who travelled the world, enjoying the social life and the business contacts every bit as much as his cricket. He later found a niche as a writer, and I had many an enjoyable hour by his side in the press-box, taking in this urbane man's wide-ranging views and recollections.

Peebles, an amateur at heart: was once listed on the scoresheet in South Africa as "absent, bathing"

A wine merchant, he invited me to his London office to partake of a well-stocked drinks cabinet and a fund of reminiscence – much of which is fortunately now logged in his books, all of which bear the hallmark of wit and good humour. He was later to apply his logical mind to trying to resolve the contentious matter of defining a throw, his book *Straight from the Shoulder* resulting.

It was absorbing to hear from his own lips how in 1930 he had benefited from the advice and encouragement of the Australian spin wizard Arthur Mailey, and how the miserable tour manager, W.L.Kelly, admonished Mailey for coaching someone from the opposition. Mailey's muttered retort was that "spin bowling is an art, and art is international". The unsmiling Kelly turned and left.

Ian Peebles had lost the sight of an eye (though the disability was scarcely noticeable) after a bomb blast in London during the war, when he was serving in MI5. There was certainly nothing "one-eyed" about his view of cricket and cricketers. This polished man cared greatly for the game.

Ian gave me his copies of *The Cricketer* from 1930-32, unbound, crumpled and proudly annotated in fountain pen in his youthful hand. In that illustrious summer of 1930 he had drawn lines beside the chronicles of his performances. He must have been excited when he read an article by the old Middlesex amateur S.W.Scott, who had written that "Peebles will be great".

His worthy deeds fell short of that rarest level but it remains an enthralling experience to study film of him bowling to Woodfull and Ponsford, Bradman and Kippax, Jackson and McCabe in that 1930 Oval Test. Throughout his 71 determined overs they never clobbered him. It was natural that I should have asked him to read through the typescript of my 1974 biography of the doomed young Archie Jackson. In his distinctively large handwriting Ian recorded his approval, adding his own heartfelt tribute to Jackson.

One day his integrity caught me off guard. I requested an obituary from him for Stewie Dempster, the great New Zealand batsman. But he declined. "I'd rather not, if you don't mind," he said. "I didn't like the chap at all."

It is hard to imagine anyone passing a judgment like that on I.A.R.Peebles.

*The Oval, August 9, 1930: Jack Hobbs scores a record-breaking run
(off Peebles), overtaking W.G.Grace's first-class aggregate of 54,896*

Wilfred Rhodes

1877-1973

He Bowled to WG and Shrewsbury

IT SEEMS almost beyond belief now that I once knew a man who was born as long ago as 1877, only a few months after the very first Test match; who played for Yorkshire in the century before last; and who talked me through his dismissal of Dr W.G.Grace. With flighty slow left-arm guile, Wilfred Rhodes took 4187 first-class wickets, a mark that will surely remain supreme. He also made close to 40,000 runs and achieved the rare 1000/100 double in Test matches against Australia.

Wilfred was now completely blind and in his 93rd year. He lived with his daughter in Canford Cliffs, Dorset, and before my pilgrimage I enquired about his preferences. "Father enjoys an occasional drink, and a bottle of sherry, Dubonnet or whisky will please him," replied Muriel.

There were some amazing treasures in that room: the ball with which he bowled Australia out for 36 at Edgbaston in 1902, another used in his 15 for 124 in a 1903-04 Melbourne Test match, a silver salver, a mounted emu egg. It broke the old man's heart when the property was later burgled.

Tape-recorder plugged in, a stupendous flight through major events and people of so long ago ensued. His voice was rasping, the product of considerable effort. But details were clearly remembered. That fuss over Clem Hill's run-out at Sydney in 1903-04 was unjustified. Wilfred knew because he was fielding in an ideal position. That was the Test in which he scored 40 not out at Number 11 and helped R.E.Foster (287) to add 130. He was very proud of that. Then, at the MCG eight years later, he opened the England innings with Jack Hobbs and they put on 323, a record against Australia to this day.

Wilfred Rhodes in his pomp: 1911-12

As for the dismissal of WG, at Hastings in 1900, he also claimed the wickets of those other champions Tom Hayward and A.E.Stoddart. Grace was lbw for 5 but just stood there. Wilfred remembered the no-nonsense umpire Bob Thoms saying: "You're out! You're out! You've got to go!" A year later Wilfred had Grace stumped, and in 1903 he bowled him for 28.

His own dismissal for 199 at Hove in 1909 still hurt, mainly because his partner Schofield Haigh had just run one run short. The 1930 memory of having Bradman missed at mid-off from his first ball was equally painful.

First-hand views on players such as Victor Trumper were precious: "Agreeable fella." Surely only Rhodes among bowlers ever actually "wanted to get at Trumper"? The pitch was damp, and, under the prevailing lbw law, Australia's skipper Joe Darling, a left-hander, was able to keep padding away at the frustrated Rhodes.

The old man explained his method: "I had flight, I'd spin and length and direction." He made it all seem so simple. After bowling Arthur Shrewsbury ("nice little fellow") he half-apologised to him: "It were a fluke!" "No, sir," replied the batsman.

That hoary old legend about George Hirst and Rhodes "getting 'em in singles" to win the Oval Test of 1902 by one wicket was hogwash. "It were some press man's invention," Wilfred confirmed. It wouldn't have made

Old, blind, but still alive with recollections: Wilfred Rhodes in his nineties, with the author

The England side at Edgbaston, 1902, which might still be regarded as the finest ever to take the field: rear – George Hirst, Dick Lilley, Bill Lockwood, Len Braund, Wilfred Rhodes; front – Charles Fry, F. Stanley Jackson, Archie MacLaren, Ranjitsinhji, Gilbert Jessop, Johnny Tyldesley

sense, would it? They might have managed a two here or a four there.

He was wearing a cardigan, and I supported his arm as he shuffled down the hallway, a soft and slack left arm that had spun out all those thousands of batsmen. "It's all curves, is Bournemouth," was his unconsciously symbolic remark as he gave me directions for the drive home. We shook hands and he felt his way back into the house. That journey was rendered no easier by misty eyes.

I returned several times to sit with him, the last when he was in a nursing-home. I'd had the pleasure of escorting him to the last of all his cricket matches, a one-dayer at Dean Park, Bournemouth. I alerted Peter West so that the TV cameras could pick him out. As the ground announcer made Wilfred's presence known to the huge gathering, the grand old veteran shakily got to his feet and doffed his hat.

Soon afterwards, in July 1973, I went to his funeral, a private affair. There could have been no more overwhelming symbol of the closing of an age than the slow disappearance of the coffin beyond the golden curtains.

Jack Robertson
1917-1996
The Gentleman Professional

THE MIDDLESEX record score of 331 not out still stands by his name. It was stroked at Worcester in 1949. But Jack Robertson's typically modest recall was simply a rueful memory. With a chuckle, he recalled discovering that evening that some uncharitable local had deflated his car tyres.

Another Robertson gem was an innings of 121 for England against New Zealand at his beloved Lord's in 1949: after which he was immediately

Jack Robertson's clean strokeplay included the hook shot, played here against Surrey

dropped. The understanding had been that he was just filling in for Len Hutton's established Test opening partner Cyril Washbrook, who had been injured.

Clean and classical of style, Jack was in one sense an "also" man. But there was no more polished batsman in England. Of course, the famous golden summer of 1947 was headlined day after day by Denis Compton and Bill Edrich, who hit 7355 runs between them in all first-class matches. For Middlesex, who were champions that year, Compton gathered 2033 runs (96.81), Edrich 2257 (77.83). Yet Jack Robertson scored 2214 (65.12, with 11 hundreds) and his opening partner Syd Brown 1709 (40.69). In all matches that season (no one-dayers then) those four batsmen gathered a phenomenal *12,193* runs. And they were all Englishmen.

First contact with Jack came in 1964. Newly landed from Sydney, where I'd been playing first-grade cricket, I took some helpful person's advice and enquired about a Middlesex trial, since I'd been born only a mile from Lord's.

You never know, there might be the odd Middlesex 2nd XI match in the offing. Jack Robertson was now county coach, one of that fine breed of men from a generation that was principled, perfectly groomed, polite and restrained, like the Army officer he'd once been. The Dunkirk evacuation in 1940 was one of the more dramatic entries on his cv. It was easy to imagine how cool and disciplined he must have been in an emergency such as no mere cricket match could ever compare.

He guided me to a net on the Nursery ground, and let loose four fast bowlers, three of them of West Indian heritage. I prodded and poked. Jack said little. Come to think of it, he might even have said nothing. It was not until several summers later that I played charity cricket with him, and had a personal close-up of his pleasing style at the crease. This was the man who had pulled a defiant six immediately after a German V1 had persuaded the players to throw themselves flat on the turf in a 1944 match at Lord's. The "buzz bomb" exploded nearby. Jack was to be less fortunate four years later when a Ray Lindwall bouncer broke his jaw.

J.D.B.Robertson, officer and gentleman, professional cricketer

Now, having accepted a beer before a Taverners dinner, he was agitated and uneasy when the formalities denied him a chance to reciprocate. What a gentleman.

Several times I went to Jack's home – which he'd cutely named Stikiwikits (it read the same backwards) – to prompt him to plough through some reminiscences. Contending with a draining illness, he reclined on the couch, and his voice was soft and rather weary. Wife Joyce brought regular sustaining cups of tea.

I borrowed and copied his 9.5mm films of tours of the Caribbean and in South Africa in the late 1940s, and also his fabulous clip of 80-year-old S.F.Barnes bowling in 1953.

Although Jack now left the house hardly at all, we persuaded him and Joyce to attend a special National Film Theatre show when the principal guest of honour was Denis Compton. It was embarrassing to realise that midst all that collection of precious footage the only piece of newsreel showing poor Jack was his dismissal by Athol Rowan. He whispered a rueful mock protest, but still enjoyed the warmth of the cinema get-together.

He was the archetypal aged cricketer: brimming with sun-lit memories, trotting off name after name, match after match, modest to a fault, and, every session, quietly enjoying those journeys down the haunting corridors of reminiscence. I wonder whether all Test cricketers in the full flush of their success recognise it for the passing phenomenon that it inevitably becomes. This man, with an average of 46 from his 11 Tests, his second century a match-saving effort in Trinidad, accepted that it had all had to end, and he exuded gratitude for what the game had given him. We are not talking about riches here – not financial anyway.

As for that net trial at Lord's, I'm just about resigned to hearing nothing further from them now.

Peter Roebuck
1956-2011
Through Shadows

FIRST SIGHT of him said it all: the thin, bespectacled teenager on the television screen stood at the batting crease on ramrod legs, back arched, his long profile replicating a question mark. Creepy.

He was a workmanlike batsman for Cambridge University and Somerset (Jim Laker said that watching him bat was like being at a requiem mass), but surely some inferior players have won Test caps, something Peter Roebuck never managed to do.

He displayed his innate determination when he was Somerset's captain, orchestrating the exit from the playing staff of Viv Richards and Joel Garner, who were soon followed out the door by an outraged Ian Botham, who labelled Roebuck "Judas". He looked so alone, leaning against the door-frame in that feverish gathering when the decision was being reached.

Having written an outstanding book or two, Roebuck set his sights on full-time journalism and broadcasting. The initial moves were in the cricket magazine world. He wrote to me (the letter is undated, but it must have been around 1990) suggesting that I may have seen his offerings in *The Cricketer*, and that he

The young Roebuck, with all before him.
An award presentation from Ted Dexter

saw no reason to be forever bound to one magazine. An article was enclosed for *Wisden Cricket Monthly*, in awful handwriting for which there was no apology.

He was my captain when the English Press played their New Zealand counterparts in Wellington, and was most solicitous when I joined him at the crease, expounding a fairly lengthy theory about how to handle John Morrison's innocent-looking slow left-armers. Morrison got him that over.

I published one or two more of Roebuck's offerings, but in what was then a rather murky world of magazine rivalry, he soon became chained to *The Cricketer*, probably on account of his Cambridge background. Thereafter he turned surprisingly unpleasant. He worked his way through the media jungle and, having left England in disgust, apparently feeling himself undervalued, he managed to set himself up in Australia with ABC Radio and a newspaper group. I saw him from time to time in the press-boxes of Brisbane and Sydney, and was surprised by his strut. Where was the humility now?

He had taken to wearing a preposterous straw hat, and constantly broke one of the press-box codes by standing up at the front, insensitive to having blocked the view for many of the occupants. To stir it further, David Gower teased him over his new "Australian" accent.

The bitter magazine competition of old was cast aside when he asked me about Archie Jackson's glorious 164 on Ashes debut at Adelaide in 1928-29. I went to the Gabba office and borrowed their copy of my 1973 biography of Jackson, and Roebuck buried himself in it for the rest of the day. When his book on Great Innings came out there was no acknowledgement to any of us who had supplied him with material. This man had a lot to learn.

In view of his knowing references to depression in one of his books, I invited him to write a foreword to *By His Own Hand*, my study of cricket's suicides. After much of his contribution had pre-empted the book's contents, he went on to write that his own earlier chronicle on his frustrations and depression had somehow brought release from the problem: "some people have predicted a gloomy end for this writer . . . It will not be so." This was widely quoted after his death.

It was not really surprising that we hardly ever saw Roebuck during the 1989 South African Test Centenary gathering. Many days and nights he went missing. It was thought that he was meeting members of the African National Congress.

His voice on Australian radio came across as – well – rather sinister. But he had his followers. He even weathered some unsavoury publicity concerning some young cricketers, his legal mind, doubtless guided by his counsel, securing a lower-level charge and suspended sentence. It began to seem that he was a great survivor.

Not without a certain sense of distraction, I found myself sitting with him and the ABC's Jim Maxwell for a lunchtime on-air discussion during the 2007 Sydney Ashes Test match. I did my stuff as best I could. But later I wondered

Cricket star caned teens

Courier-Mail 21-10-01

Roebuck guilty on three counts

By BRUCE WILSON
In London

CRICKET commentator and former county captain Peter Roebuck has been given suspended jail sentences after pleading guilty to caning teenage cricketers he had been coaching.

Roebuck is an ABC broadcaster.

A Crown Court in Somerset, the English county Roebuck once captained, heard he beat his pupils on the buttocks for misdemeanours such as not running fast enough.

The young men were "terrified" of Roebuck, prosecutor Ian Fenny told the court.

Roebuck was sentenced to four months' jail on each of three counts of assault causing actual bodily harm in 1999.

The sentences were suspended for two years and he was ordered to pay costs of about $2400.

Roebuck, 45, who pleaded not guilty, said he intended to return to Australia to resume his ca-

reer with ABC radio and as a writer for The Sydney Morning Herald and Melbourne's The Age.

Mr Fenny told the court Roebuck would not coach British players because they were not mentally tough enough. He chose the three South Africans because he thought they were from a culture that accepted corporal punishment.

He met Keith Whiting, Reginald Keats and Henk Lindeque, all 19, while working as a commentator and invited them to live at his home, subject to "house rules".

After one training session, during which Whiting had failed to keep up on a run, Roebuck caned him on the buttocks, over his clothes. Later, he consoled the teenager and asked to see the marks he had caused. Mr Fenny said there

were similar incidents with Keats and Lindeque.

Roebuck said his life had been "hell" since the offences came to light, when one of the cricketers showed his welts to the secretary of a nearby cricket club, who passed the matter to police.

He accepted the court's decision but said he had not detected unhappiness among the boys.

"Obviously I misjudged the mood and that was my mistake and my responsibility and I accept that," he said. "I accept that I have been given a second chance. I am very keen to take it."

Defence lawyer Paul Mendelle said Roebuck was a "complex man" who set high standards for himself and expected them of others, and who had used corporal punishment for the sole purpose of encouraging the teenagers.

HOUSE RULES: Commentator Peter Roebuck

The somewhat unpredictable and tragic end

how the devil I could have let Peter Roebuck get away with his absurd claim that the ICC branded only Asian bowlers as chuckers, a typical left-field line, in keeping with his ongoing need to stun his audience or readership. I should have challenged it. That was the last time I was to see or hear him.

After he leapt to his death in Cape Town in 2011, as unsavoury rumours circulated, I couldn't help but picture the slender, vulnerable lad in glasses, patting the crease with his bat, threatening no serious harm to any bowler, but radiating grim determination. How could somebody so solitary and introverted go out later into the world and carve out a media career for himself? Perhaps, if nothing else, and in spite of his personality flaws, he deserves credit for beguiling so many sports editors with his supposed insights.

Andy Sandham
1890-1982
Scorer of the First Test 300

NOBODY IN that smoky pub in Clapham could have had the slightest inkling that the little old chap in the corner, quietly sipping a beer, was the scorer of the first-ever Test match treble-hundred. Andy Sandham, warm under his raincoat, was now seeing a depleted version of the world around him through thick-lensed glasses. Those eyes had once assessed the best bowling up and down England and on foreign shores.

It was south London in 1978. He was 87 and feeling it. Discomfort seemed to have been a companion all through life. He recalled the injuries, illnesses and pain that befell him during his long career (1911-1937). To this day he shares three Surrey record partnerships: the 173 with Andy Ducat for the tenth wicket came at Leyton after a bout of food poisoning; his 282 not out at Old Trafford in 1928 was curtailed by something close to pleurisy; on a tour of South Africa he was badly knocked about in a car crash; and during the First

Doing his bit in the First World War: Andy Sandham with Surrey team-mate Bill Hitch (left)

World War he was repatriated after an appendix operation just before the Royal Fusiliers went into battle at Delville Wood.

The most amusing of Sandy's discomforts, though, came during that 325 for England against West Indies at Kingston early in 1930. He had talked me through it during an earlier meeting at his flat, recalling that with his spare bats all broken or sold as the tour neared conclusion, and his remaining one cracked, he borrowed from his captain, Freddie Calthorpe. "It was not a bat I would have chosen myself. It was a long-handle. That's it over there." And sure enough this precious dark relic was propped up in the corner.

With Patsy Hendren, Sandham, in his elegant panama hat, resumes his marathon innings in Jamaica in 1930, on the way to the first Test triple-century

He painted a hilarious picture of that innings. George Gunn, aged 50, was carelessly out for 85. Andy lamented that it would have been nice to have made a Test century at Gunn's age. Gunn retorted: "I thought if one of us didn't get out we wouldn't catch the boat home!" The vessel, Sandham recalled, wasn't due to sail for another ten days. He batted on and on, and by halfway through the second day he had to contend with fresh young batsmen like Les Ames wanting quick singles. "Now look here, Les," he said, "it's all right for you but I've been in for hours and I'm in my fortieth year."

Another problem was that he had needed to borrow Patsy Hendren's boots, and one kept slipping off as he scuttled singles. At 325 he played on – "Bless me!" – to Herman Griffith. England made 849, bowled West Indies out for 286, and batted again.

Calthorpe took pity on Sandham and put him in at No.7 this time. He made 50. "I believe even now that's the record for most runs in a Test match." I deeply regret having then told him that Greg Chappell had recently surpassed that 375. A flicker of regret touched his old countenance.

Andrew Sandham was proud of his opening association with the charming Jack Hobbs. "He was a great man, Jack. We were together for many, many,

many years, and I think twice there was a run-out." What about the newspaper placards proclaiming a Hobbs duck on an afternoon when Sandham made a hundred? "It used to annoy my wife."

The high points included his 100th century, on a damp Basingstoke pitch in 1935: he had even hit Stuart Boyes for six ("I was not built for hitting sixes, you know"). He reached the glittering milestone with a flick behind square, hoping like mad that Boyes at short leg hadn't crept squarer, as he often did. Then there was his record 428 for the first wicket with Hobbs against Oxford University, and an unbeaten 292 against Northamptonshire. He still seemed faintly miffed at Percy Fender's declaration.

His greatest regret was that he played only five Test innings against Australia for a mere 49 runs, highest score 21 on Ashes debut at The Oval in 1921. "A snorter from McDonald finished me . . . my off stump went over and over and over. Beautiful bowler."

And Sandy himself, during all those long-ago summers, was a neat, calm and admirable sight at the crease or in the outfield. He died in 1982, aged 91, and it warms me still to think that I once shared a pint or two with him.

The prolific drive: Sandham registered
41,284 runs in his 1000 first-class innings

E.J. "Tiger" Smith
1886-1979
A Brummie's Tales

DURING THE 1970s a powerful incentive to visit Edgbaston was the tough old creature who held court in the players' tea-room. Ernest John "Tiger" Smith, wicketkeeper in Warwickshire's first Championship-winning side in 1911 and for England in a triumphant Ashes series the following winter, used to park himself on a seat like some great bear, walking-stick across his knee, gnarled fist attached to a slowly emptying beer glass. For all his 80-odd years, like many a veteran of the early part of the 20th Century, he had a rich fund of stories, and for as long as you cared to listen he would roll them out, one hard on the other.

What a start to his maiden Test: S.F.Barnes had that spell of 5 for 6 on the opening day at Melbourne, with Tiger standing up at the stumps, catching Armstrong midst the carnage, then holding further catches off the bowling of Bill Hitch, Johnny Douglas, and his county skipper F.R.Foster. Replacing Strudwick after the first Test, Smith was naturally preferred by Foster, a fast left-armer who swung it into leg stump, for they worked together rather like Underwood (at lesser pace) and Knott of a later generation.

Portrait taken during England's highly successful tour of Australia 1911-12

Tiger thus played in four winning Tests – albeit with a tally of byes (94) against his name that might be of comfort to Matthew Prior. What mattered was a compliment paid him by the legendary old Australian wicketkeeper Jack Blackham.

The Ashes won, England then carried all before them in the 1912 Triangular Series at home, with Tiger holding his Test place with some brave keeping on some tricky pitches, 96 byes skidding and leaping past him in the six Tests. And how could he forget the stitches to his lip after both a ball bowled by Barnes and Herby Taylor's bat smashed into it simultaneously?

For the tour of South Africa (no F.R.Foster now) little Strudwick reclaimed the premier wicketkeeping position, with Smith earning one further cap at Johannesburg in 1913-14 as a tailend batsman and fielder. Played 11, won 9, drawn 2: a Test record of which to be very proud.

And he was. In that rasping Brummie accent he spoke admiringly of Trumper and Hill and Macartney, moving on to other tours such as the 1925-26 romp to the West Indies, which sparked a couple of unprintable stories. He would flick across a long and eventful county career: nearly 500 matches for his native Warwickshire, 20 centuries and almost 900 dismissals, 153 of them stumpings as he stood up fearlessly, even to the briskest. As I picture the old bruiser now I'm tempted to believe that he would have growled: "Stand back for Harmison? Not on your life!"

An old man dreams: "Tiger" by the entrance to Edgbaston cricket ground. The plaque marks the place where his old mate S.F.Barnes's ashes are interred (Ken Kelly)

Then there was the umpiring through the 1930s (eight Tests): he lowered his voice to tell me that he rendered black trousers popular, the simple reason being that if the bladder misbehaved while he stood at square leg, nobody would notice. His most significant decision came when it was discovered that Sutcliffe and Holmes might not have broken the first-wicket record of 554 after all, merely equalled it. Tiger instantly, and conveniently, remembered calling a no-ball early in the day, and checked the scorebook. Sure enough the scorers had somehow missed it. So the new record of 555 was confirmed. He seemed proud of that.

His opinions were refreshingly frank. Why shouldn't they have been? Bob Wyatt irritated him. Hobbs and Hammond impressed him deeply. So did the thunderous little hitter Jessop, and George Gunn. Percy Jeeves, he believed, would have played for England had the Great War not claimed him. He deplored the hypocrisy of many of the amateurs, who made far too much money from the game. What fun Tiger would have had in this po-faced age, with that pompous word "inappropriate" lurking round every corner.

Tiger Smith gave his whole life to cricket. After playing and umpiring he became Warwickshire's coach, sharing further success with the 1951 County Championship. He died in 1979 and his ashes were scattered across the Edgbaston turf. Where might those ashes be now? (Compton's and Edrich's were cast to the Lord's outfield, which was later dug up.) Tiger probably wouldn't have cared a jot.

Ernest James "Tiger" Smith, tough-guy wicketkeeper

Sydney Smith junior
1880-1972
Close-up of the Punch-up

EARLY IN 1972, by arrangement, I went to see a very old man at his home on Sydney's North Shore. He was practically bed-ridden, but his mind was still clear, and his memories stretched way back to the lost years before the First World War. Syd Smith junior, a Public Service employee, had been an *honorary* cricket administrator for most of his life: for his club as a youngster, then as long-term secretary ("chief executive officer" in today's high-flown terminology) of the New South Wales Cricket Association, and then as treasurer, eventually serving as president for thirty years until he was 86. He also served the Australian Cricket Board (honorary secretary 1911-1927), altogether a matchless record in the history of the game. He had been a player too, although only in the lower grades.

He seemed to have been an eternal presence, forever visible in boardroom photographs and presentation line-ups on the SCG turf. Tons of paper must have passed across his desk through years untold. And here he was, a pale, serious, gnome-like figure in the quiet solitude of his solid old home, marooned with his memories of cricketers, places and events.

As a competent speaker as well as bookkeeper he had been appointed manager of the 1921 and 1926 Australian tours of Britain. He produced a handsome book on the first of these, and caused the players to fume by asking them to pay for their copies. I got him to sign my own. By all accounts he had been a shrewd and conscientious manager, charging the public for watching the Australians at net practice, but seeing to it that the players remembered always that they were representatives of their country. A large tour profit was recorded both times.

On my second visit, he agreed to sell me some of his old cricket books and pictures. In addition, because the Frith family were shortly due to sail back to England, I offered to buy his old cabin trunk, which still had Otranto and Canadian Pacific and Ashes labels attached. It stands in the garage to this day, a bulky oddity as cricket memorabilia goes.

But if Syd Smith was remembered for anything in particular it was for being a central figure in the painful "Big Six" row of 1911-12, when Trumper, Hill, Armstrong, Cotter, Ransford and Carter refused terms to tour England, leaving the Board to send a much-reduced side. As Board secretary, Syd Smith was at the centre of this upheaval, and it was now my good fortune to listen to his first-hand – one might almost say "fist-hand" – account of the machinations. When the climax was reached – the eye-witness recall of the punch-up between Clem Hill and the virtuous Peter McAlister in the Board's office in Martin Place, Sydney – I got out my pencil and paper and noted the

Syd Smith jnr (standing, left) with the NSWCA executive committee during the stormy Australian summers of 1910-11 and 1911-12. Also standing are secretary Percy Bowden and H.G.Hewlett; front: Colin Sinclair, chairman W.P.McElhone and A.W.Green

nonagenarian's recollection carefully.

Mr Smith had just provided the two selectors with the names of available players when the pair started arguing. Hill ended up shouting to McAlister that he'd been "looking for a bloody punch in the jaw all night". And he gave him one. They wrestled, and Hill had McAlister by the throat near the open window, three floors up. Smith and Frank Iredale tried to restrain them. "McAlister was in a bad way, bleeding copiously. It took some time for Iredale and myself to get him presentable."

With a rare glimmer of humour, the old man continued: "This was my first experience of Test selection, and I was somewhat shocked, especially as

The final portrait: a snapshot of Sydney Smith taken by the author on his last visit

the two concerned were most likable men." He then recalled that in 1909 McAlister had been punched by another "anti-Board man". Oh, what a grey, sedate cricket age we're living through today.

Clem Hill was soon handing Syd Smith his resignation as selector, and Smith tried to keep the brawl secret. But it was in the *Sydney Morning Herald* next day. Hill had leaked the story.

"It's been a long life, and an interesting one," Syd Smith reflected huskily, "but thank goodness it hasn't all been that interesting." The 1912 dispute had distressed him, and as Board secretary, close to all the players, he had done his best to bring the sides together. But there were some very strong and wilful characters involved in this stormy cricket chapter.

It was a thrill to shake the hand of the man who had shaken all their hands and had seen so much cricket history carved out, some of it blood-spattered.

Herbert Strudwick
1880-1970
Tea and Tom Richardson

OF ALL the countless cricketers' hands I've shaken, Herbert Strudwick's was by far the most disfigured, with broken knuckles twisted and swollen from the impact of thousands upon thousands of balls fired at him by a long succession of bowlers stretching back to England's mighty 1890s fast bowler Tom Richardson, and by Struddy's dear friend Jack Hobbs in the covers. A small chap of about Tim Ambrose's size, Struddy would play on in agony from chipped bones, fearing that another keeper might take his place in the Surrey or England team. (No, he never did put raw steak in his gloves: but he admitted that the best way to break in a new pair was to soak them in urine.)

Refusing to be overwhelmed: Bert Strudwick welcomes the Frith family to his home in Shoreham-by-Sea

A widower when I went to see him, living alone in Shoreham-by-Sea, Bert Strudwick was missing Hobbs, who had lived in retirement just along the coast until his recent death in 1963. After years of mateship in Surrey and England colours, they had long been golfing partners. Now in his mid-eighties, the little keeper would brew a pot of tea and bring in some cakes and photo albums to the cosy little sitting-room. With the electric fire glowing, the memories flowed: what a grump was Tom Hayward, how unnerving it was to field as a substitute in a Test match at silly point to Victor Trumper, what a thrill it had been to receive encouragement from the legendary old Australian wicketkeeper Jack Blackham, how nasty it was facing Jack Gregory's thunderbolts aimed at the collarbone.

Struddy's kindly blue eyes sparkled as he recalled a prank on the voyage to Australia in 1903 (first of his four tours there). MCC captain Plum Warner was in a cabin with his fiancee, Agnes. Mischievous Struddy tapped on the porthole and ran for his life. Simple fun like that kept everybody happy – apart

211

from Mr Warner.

There was a sour note on his next tour of Australia. The Warwickshire left-arm fast bowler Frank Foster wanted E.J. "Tiger" Smith, his county keeper, in the Test side, so he blatantly embarrassed Smith's rival Strudwick by signalling that he would send the next ball down the leg side for a stumping. As the little Surrey man moved to his left, Foster fired the ball straight to Frank Woolley at first slip.

Born in Mitcham, South London, in 1880, Strudwick started with Surrey on £1 a week, and finished in 1927 with a then world-record tally of 1496 dismissals (254 of them stumpings), a figure unmatched for almost 50 years until John Murray became No.1 for a time. The last of Struddy's 28 Tests was that classic Ashes contest at his beloved Oval in 1926, when, at 46, he kept wicket to a glittering array of bowlers in Larwood, Tate, Geary, Stevens and the 48-year-old master spinner Rhodes. England manoeuvred towards a 289-run victory which he still remembered clearly and with poignant pride. If only he could relive it all. Thinking about it was the next-best thing.

Back in 1902, W.G.Grace bowled him for 0 at Crystal Palace, having offered him an easy ball to avoid the "pair". Struddy didn't mind. His heart had been set on racing over to watch the FA Cup final replay at the nearby Crystal

"Struddy" at home behind the stumps as Australia's mighty allrounder Jack Gregory larrups another ball through the cover field during the 1926 Ashes series

Palace football ground. Two years earlier, when he was 20, he faced the first West Indian side to visit England, making a stumping off the fast bowler Neville Knox and finding the overweight Tom Richardson a terrible handful as he cut the ball way down the leg side, with pace and bounce.

Small and brave behind the stumps, Strudwick was a Surrey favourite, and there was nothing the crowd enjoyed more than when he scampered after a ball turned down to long leg, where fieldsmen rarely stood in those days: "I always seemed to be running faster than I really was," he said. His short legs created the illusion.

His third tour of Australia, in 1920-21, was the roughest. England lost 0-5. But Struddy didn't play in all five Tests. Arthur Dolphin of Yorkshire was generously given a chance in the fourth, at Melbourne (his only Test appearance as a player: he subsequently umpired in several).

The modern non-stop squawking from behind the stumps would have horrified Bert Strudwick. He was a sportsman and a gentleman, typical of his generation. And he also knew how to brew a perfect cup of tea.

Popular, long-serving Surrey and England keeper Strudwick

Herbert Sutcliffe
1894-1978
Not a Hair Out of Place

AS SURVIVING film testifies, Herbert Sutcliffe was not exactly poetry in motion. He even ran stiff-leggedly. But he was a model of sound technique, control and poise, usually capless, not a hair out of place, and he regularly batted for hours at a time. In fact to this day no batsman who has played as many as his 54 Tests touches his average of 60.73.

They became part of the English language: Hobbs (in cap) and Sutcliffe, almost as reliable as the Bank of England itself

His suavity and grace were instantly apparent upon first sight of him in person, outside The Oval before that memorable Ashes Test of 1968, forty-two years after a classic in which he himself had steered England to victory over Australia with a skillful 161 on a damp pitch. I used to carry a massive book into which many hundreds of cricketers were persuaded to sign their names. Here was a big one.

Mr Sutcliffe was charming: "I'm sure we've met before?" We had never met and he probably knew it. Out came the fountain pen and into the book went a valued signature, clear and bold. He was encouraged to think back to that 1926 Test match, which he did with modesty, and for the rest of the day – the rest of the year for that matter – I was aglow from that chance encounter with a true immortal.

We corresponded and at his request I was able to locate a few copies of his old book *For England and Yorkshire*. Back came a large photograph of Sutcliffe and his friend Jack Hobbs going out to bat. They seemed then, as they seem now, despite all the later challengers, to be the ultimate in opening partnerships, part of the language.

Herbert Sutcliffe was no sensationalist: "The reason for my two car accidents," he wrote in 1971, "was a burst blood vessel over the left eye which impaired my vision and a black-out followed." Even in old age he allowed nothing to fluster him. The film evidence is still there: a Jack Gregory bouncer, a parry or a sway, a contemplative walk around the crease; elsewhere a sudden break from his stance as somebody moved behind the bowler: an imperious wave of the hand before resumption. As a senior pro during the

*The cool and prolific Sutcliffe swings a ball to leg, Australians Bert Oldfield
(wicketkeeper) and Jack Gregory left to hope*

red-hot Bodyline series, still mindful of the battering dished out by Australia in earlier years, it was often he – ahead of captain Douglas Jardine's instruction – who ushered England's leg-side cordon into position after a few new-ball overs from Larwood and Voce.

This was the man who, in 1924-25, scored three centuries in his first two Ashes Tests and went on piling up runs for Yorkshire and England between the two world wars, one of only seven batsmen to finish with over 50,000.

Late in life he relished his role as man-of-the-match adjudicator at one-day games. At Old Trafford it was my good fortune to be his sponsor's "guide" for the day. It worked out at roughly forty minutes of rich reminiscence for every gin and tonic. He talked about "dear Jack" (Hobbs, not Gregory) and of the gratification in playing for those powerful Yorkshire teams. He was concerned about the hook shot employed by England's latest bright hope Frank Hayes, wanted to discuss the shot with him, but would wait until invited. "I could play the hook," he murmured without a trace of boastfulness.

Suddenly he disclosed that his wife had just died in a nursing-home, her dress ignited by her cigarette. They had been married for a very long time. He sank into a reflective quiet.

His presentation duties now loomed as a big problem. The pavilion steps were wet and slippery, with a maze of television cables on the ground. With his arthritic knees and walking-sticks it would be far too treacherous for him to attempt to enter the field to announce the match award.

I tried hard to persuade him to stay in the pavilion. He would have none of it. He was being paid to perform certain duties and he would carry them out to the letter. We feared a fall and worse.

Mercifully the match was suspended until next day, so no presentations were called for. But I had witnessed at close hand the immense grittiness of Herbert Sutcliffe, as brave and unrelenting at eighty as fifty years before.

E.W.Swanton

1907-2000

Shoulder to Hip

THE FIRST cricket book I ever bought was *Elusive Victory*, E.W.Swanton's magisterial account of the 1950-51 Ashes series, during which I had my first "living" sample of cricket's greatest contest. Years later, at Lord's, I approached the great man, and after a pleasantry delivered in that deep, rich voice he inscribed the book "Jim Swanton". This suggested that he was in a relaxed mood, for his initials were usually his insignia, almost in the "HRH" class.

Most said that he was overbearing and pompous, a view endorsed by his mean treatment of an Aussie journalist in the press-box that very day. The poor chap needed to shout down a faint telephone line to Sydney. This disturbed the Lord of the Press-box, who dispatched one of his acolytes to instruct the frustrated reporter to lower his voice.

"Now look here, David." The apprentice awaits his next order

Small wonder, then, that in 1972 I was quaking in my boots at the prospect of being interviewed by EWS as a prospective deputy editor of *The Cricketer*. It would be nothing formal, just a "chat" on the press-box balcony during the Oval Test. We both knew it was an interview, but still it proceeded as a friendly exchange, the great man probing my knowledge of cricket, assessing my affection for it, and no doubt my literacy too. He seemed pleased that half my life had been spent in Sydney. He knew Australia well, liked it, and had spent those unspeakable war years in Changi camp with British and Australian prisoners.

I scored points with the reminder that I'd just tracked down the mighty 1920s Australian cricketer Jack Gregory, a recluse, and a great favourite of his. It was going well. Then he asked if I knew who Jimmy Cannon was. "Oh, he was 'Tityrus', who wrote *Wickets and Goals*," came the confident reply. "No, no, no!" roared EWS. "That was Catton! Cannon was chief clerk at Lord's for forty years!" He was chuckling.

With that, I think I secured the job.

Although he never was a father, he could be fatherly. It was agreed that I could call him "Jim". I did all the editorial work. He dished out orders. No sweep shot to be featured in the magazine – least of all on the front cover. (Too late: see Tony Lewis breaking the rule, February 1973 edition.) Once, in a swaying taxi, we tried to agree which picture to use for the next front cover. It struck me as a bizarre way for a magazine to be edited. His missives zoomed in from Sandwich by first-class post, or via sepulchral phone-calls. He was always delightfully polite to my wife.

In his Grandstand box at Lord's for his 200th Test match he was the life and soul of the party. In came Brian Johnston. "Aha!" roared Jim, "here's Big Nose Johnston!" Then the reminiscences: the astonishing recall of having W.G.Grace pointed out to him around 1910 as he sat in his pram; enchanted by every run of Bradman's 254 on this very ground in 1930; and so on.

For me the most amusing expression, frequently used, was "Now look heah!" It was his way of asserting himself, an attempted rib-crusher. I hoped it would come in useful when I needed him as an ally when Gordon Ross, his own *Playfair Cricket Monthly* having been absorbed by *The Cricketer* in 1973, was trying to cling to the power he'd just lost. I rang Jim and told him that our former rival was insisting that all his regulars be accommodated in our magazine.

"David," said my editorial director, "we must stand shoulder to shoulder!" Since he was half-a-foot taller than I, a comical vision came my way, and a lot of the pressure was removed from the situation.

He let me down some years later when the proprietor showed me the door, even if it turned into a blessing. And just before he died I invited Jim Swanton to the annual film show at the National Film Theatre, where his evocative hour-long film on the 1950-51 Ashes series, *Elusive Victory*, was the main feature. The audience (they cannot have known he was wearing red socks) gave him a thunderous ovation. I told him that not even Denis Compton the previous year had generated such a reception, a remark which caused the nonagenarian to beam from ear to ear. It was a warming goodbye.

A knighthood would have been pleasant, but
E.W.Swanton CBE will do nicely

Fred Trueman
1931-2006
"It woan't coom out, son!"

CERTAIN EVENTS are vividly dated in memory by cricket incidents. Mum went in for an operation in 1952. I have always dated that long-ago event through an article in a magazine in the hospital waiting room. It told of the dramatic emergence of a fiery and truly fast bowler for England. With his swagger, luxuriant black hair, glowering features, and powerful, rhythmic run-up, Freddie Trueman was a thrilling sight on the giant newsreel screen.

Another 1958-59 photograph by the author, who was told by Freddie Trueman that it wouldn't come out. Much gratitude that it did

At long last England had somebody to put the wind up the opposition. It had been a very long wait.

He wasn't to make it to Australia for another six years. Then, here at last was the burly, vocal Yorkie in the flesh, fielding down at long leg by the white SCG pickets. I pointed my new Voigtlander at him and asked for a smile. "It woan't coom out, son!" he teased. It did.

So my personal agonies of the Hutton versus Lindwall duels were now superceded by the stomach-churning O'Neill versus Trueman battles. And four years later FST was in town again. I must admit I went off him when he brushed past the excited greeting of my mother and my wife as they chanced upon him, recognisable behind his sunglasses, hurrying from the team hotel into a taxi. But during 30 subsequent years in England I came to know Fred well and found him very likable. He was also a particularly interesting study.

For all his fame and achievements, which had extended profitably into showbusiness activities, there seemed to be an insecurity about him, as if he needed constant reassurance that he was somebody special. And, seldom revealed, he had compassion. One Test match morning at The Oval an elderly man lost control of his little car and crashed it against the steps at the rear of the pavilion. As passers-by abused the flustered driver for his clumsiness, Fred's reaction was different: "Poor old booger. Are y'all right, laad?" His concern was genuine.

When he chaired an awards panel for Captain of the Month, I proposed the skipper of the touring Australian Aboriginals team, who had had a good run recently. Everyone else around the table opposed this. Only county captains had previously been considered for the award. But Fred liked the idea, nobody felt like arguing, and so it was happily adopted.

Perhaps the most vivid abiding memory is of a long chat under bright moonlight, after some dinner or other at the Headingley ground. As the range of topics moved on to financial security, FST concluded his musings on money with a positive statement (not that he was ever capable of anything less): "I'm a millionaire, y'know." Pause. "Oh aye, I'm a millionaire." He stood there on the asphalt, a bear-like figure in the silvery back-lighting, clearly gratified at this rather naïve self-reassurance.

In 1982, eighteen years after he'd become the first to take 300 Test wickets, I came within a whisker of batting against him. Back in 1964 he had been tired. And he was tired now. Playing against the Old England XI at Harrogate, I went in just as he had taken himself off. Feeling relief but also disappointment, I had to make do with facing Titmus, Allen, D'Oliveira and Dexter, while keeping a wary eye on the sweating Fred and wondering, with a mix of trepidation and hope, whether he might give himself another over or two. One thing I realised I shared with Norm O'Neill was a propensity for sweaty nervousness on the big occasion where F.S.Trueman was concerned. When Fred looked across, winked, and said, "All right, laad?" I managed a smile, and was even tempted to ask him to take that tent-like sweater off and have a bowl at me. I regret lacking the nerve.

The last time I saw him was at the 2006 Wisden dinner. He was now 75, and looking rather dishevelled. His doctor, he said, had found nothing to explain his pain and discomfort. A few weeks later he was dead. The most colourful identity of the age was no more. It was one of the saddest realities to reconcile. Still, I've got a cluster of memories and also that precious photograph to remember him by.

"Fiery Freddie" in full flight

Cyril Walters

1905-1992

The Matinee Idol

NUMBER 31 in the John Player cigarette card series *Cricketers 1934* bears a colour portrait of a man who might just as well have been part of the *Film Stars* set, alongside Errol Flynn and Douglas Fairbanks jnr. With his dark wavy hair, kindly yet rugged features, cream cravat at his throat, Cyril Walters is a picture of elegance, an elegance that happened to express itself not only in his gentlemanly manner but in his beautiful batsmanship.

In 2009 England gained their first Lord's Test victory over Australia for 75 years. The previous instance, way back in 1934, is known as Verity's match (the Yorkshire left-arm spinner took 15 for 104), but C.F. Walters opened England's batting with Herbert Sutcliffe and scored a handsome 82 on the opening day,

The Rest 1934, a gathering of top English names: standing – Eddie Paynter, Jim Langridge, Bill Bowes, Ken Farnes, Arthur Mitchell, Charles Barnett; seated – George Duckworth, Cyril Walters, Maurice Turnbull, Walter Robins, Bryan Valentine

and a newspaper picture showing him leaping out to drive during that wristy innings is almost a replica of that famous Trumper photograph.

Just as evidence of Walters' satin-smooth leg glances and of his style and poise at the crease is safely if elusively stored in film vaults, so my memories of some privileged times with him in later life remain special and gratifying.

Although he was a quiet and dignified man, his opinions were firm and persuasive. As I sat with him at Bob Wyatt's 90th birthday lunch, Walters was encouraged to reflect on D.R.Jardine, to whom he had been vice-captain on England's 1933-34 tour of India: "I never understood the fellow. During the tour he seemed always to have a large book tucked under his arm. When the Indian officials and others lined up as he walked into a reception, one of those in the group was an uncle. You could tell, too, for he had the same huge nose as Douglas. Douglas just walked straight past him."

To Walters, bad manners were unforgivable. But he did permit himself another dart at Jardine. Against Amar Singh, a very fast, swerving Indian bowler who cut the ball back off the matting pitch, Walters was playing off the back foot with great determination. Uncharacteristically, Jardine was upset and was bowled second ball, lunging well forward. "He said he was sick of watching me play back all the time," said Cyril, with something close to a smirk.

C.F.Walters in later life

In Wyatt's absence, Walters actually led England on his Ashes debut at Trent Bridge in 1934. From his 11 Tests overall he averaged a creditable 52.26, having dealt with the challenges of Martindale, Constantine and Herman Griffith, and Wall, Grimmett and O'Reilly. The last-named told him that he thought he was England's best batsman in 1934. C.F.Walters remarkably stroked seven half-centuries in his 18 Test innings, together with a century at Madras. Among his reflections, which were always thoughtful, was that Bradman was vulnerable on pitches that were less than perfect. But he took careful note of the great Australian's assertion to him: that it was vital to keep perfectly still until the bowler releases the ball.

Through the 1920s and 1930s Cyril Walters played many charming innings for Glamorgan and then Worcestershire, with the Gravesend audience in 1933 privy to his highest score of 226. Yet his enchanting batsmanship left him with a first-class average 40 percent lower than his Test figure, dragged down by modest early Glamorgan performances. He was captain and secretary at Worcester for the first half of the 1930s before suddenly walking away from the first-class game, granting preference to marriage and business, just as the nabobs at Lord's were apparently pencilling him in to lead England on the approaching 1936-37 tour of Australia.

By the time I paid him a visit at his home in Droitwich he was a widower, and although his manner remained unwaveringly courteous, some of the elegance had faded. The reminiscences were still there to be evoked, but he seemed tired. Later, in 1986, having moved back to Wales, he wrote a postcard which concluded: "I can hardly believe that more than 50 years have passed since those carefree happy days."

Carefree? Happy? I wonder how many of today's star cricketers will one day feel quite that way?

A short-lived but effective England opening partnership:
Cyril Walters and Herbert Sutcliffe (left)

E.M. Wellings

1909-1992

Cricket's Welfare Paramount

E.M.WELLINGS (1909-92) was fortunate to be spared cricket's 21st century problems, for those of the 20th gave him quite enough about which to rage, both in conversation and in print. Between 1938 and 1973 he wrote for the old London paper the *Evening News*, his views and standards shaped at Cheltenham College and Oxford University and as an amateur for Surrey in the 1930s, one who counted himself privileged to be sharing a cricket field with Jack Hobbs and other worthy heroes. He had an acute insight into this complex game, and cared deeply for its welfare. Eventually he saw himself as a kind of guardian of its standards. There was no shortage of cricket people upon whom to unload his wrath.

Press conference, Australia 1954-55: Lyn Wellings is at the rear (right of centre); Bruce Harris (silver hair) stands in front of him; Tom Goodman is top left; Ray Robinson is in front of Goodman and to his right; Geoffrey Howard, MCC/England manager, is in dark suit, addressing the gathering

The first of my many sessions with Lyn (short for Evelyn) was over lunch during the classic Oval Test of 1968. The equally forbidding J.M.Kilburn was also at the table. They reminisced over the good times and glories of the 1930s, leaving me to wonder if it really was worthwhile to stay in cricket. I vowed I would never glorify the old days at the expense of modern times when I was as old as these gentlemen, a vow which, of course, is sometimes forgotten.

Already I knew of Wellings's tantrums: sticking a rude word on the press-box window to deter an intrusive TV camera, hurling a typewriter, stacking his running reports into a pile in the absence of a copy boy until a frantic sports editor hastened to supply one. He hated inefficiency, hypocrisy, corruption and, most of all, anything that sullied the games he loved, cricket and golf. The latter, of course, has never been the breeding ground for maladministration and player misbehaviour on cricket's scale.

Wellings on tour, in warmer climes

He covered nine tours of Australia, his favourite country, flying eastwards whenever possible to avoid jet-lag. In 1958-59, while others remained silent, he showed courage in attacking the blatantly dodgy actions of several Australian bowlers. Twelve years later he supported Ray Illingworth during England's successful Ashes challenge while it was being undermined by those who had wanted Colin Cowdrey to be captain. Wellings's tour books were all much to the point, and his last book, *Vintage Cricketers* (1983), is packed with anecdote, insight and good sense. He was not a pretentious writer, no lyrical Cardus. He dealt solely in fact and considered opinion.

And he seemed to relish swimming against the current. He detested pomposity, intrigue and bad cricket, and instinctively lashed out against these things. His independence of thought was surely the source of his energy – and sporadic unpopularity. His sometime room-mate on tour, Alex Bannister, put Lyn's tetchiness down to his lonely boyhood and public school education. The irascible old man had probably been an irascible young man.

He feared nobody, not even the Duke of Norfolk, who rebuked him publicly after he'd been critical of aspects of the 1962-63 tour of Australia under Ted Dexter's captaincy and the Duke's management. Wellings' response was that he was willing to risk incarceration in the Tower of London for upholding the right of a writer to criticise in matters of public interest. Voltaire would have been proud of him.

In retirement, E.M.Wellings and second wife Vel spent some years in Spain. That played nicely into the hands of his adversaries, who chortled that Lyn had always been "to the right of Franco". Returning to live in modest accommodation near Basingstoke, he was glad of the chance to write for *Wisden Cricket Monthly*. On one visit I was impressed by the vertical arm of a 75-year-old as he demonstrated his bowling action. The occasional reader's letter of protest drifted in, much to our amusement. Always he kept cricket's welfare paramount. This was the basis of the bond between us.

He gave Vel instructions to inform me of his death. Nothing was to be made public until after she had cast his ashes into the English Channel, on the French side. There were only five at his funeral including the minister, who asked, as we entered the chapel, if I'd say a few words. How could such a long cricket and journalistic career best be summed up? My recall is of trying to encapsulate it in a summary of his playing and his journalism, conveying too the cardinal fact: that Lyn Wellings was always very much his own man. It's a very rare quality.

Frank Woolley
1887-1978
Kentish Saint

FRANK WOOLLEY'S name is seldom mentioned in these obsessively modern days. He was a towering and immensely popular left-hander for over thirty years until 1938, possessed of a languid style which was fascinating even beyond his matchless set of figures ("Woolley causes batting to appear the easiest pastime in the world," purred Cardus). Mostly for Kent and England, he scored more first-class runs (58,969) than anyone bar Jack Hobbs. Only six stand above him in the centuries list – with Graeme Hick closing in on his 145. [Hick finished with 136 first-class hundreds.]

Seen early as a successor to Colin Blythe, Woolley also took 2068 wickets.

The widowed Woolley found late-in-life happiness with Martha

And no other fieldsman has held 1000 catches. He was a Kentish saint, and I felt profound awe when I met him in 1976.

Frank was in his 90th year, tall, white-haired, still erect, but seriously ill. Age and poor health were reasons enough to be less than exuberant, though it seems he had always been inclined towards pessimism. Through our times together at Lord's and at the hotel where he and his perky second wife, American-born Martha, were staying it emerged that money was also a problem.

In a long and eventful career his 64 Test matches were spread over 25 years. Yet somehow it was the 235 that he'd put on with Arthur Fielder for Kent's tenth wicket at Stourbridge in 1909 that initially caught the fancy.

The long-hidden details came out. Worcestershire quickie Ted Arnold had cut Woolley's lip and forced him to retire. Returning to the crease later, he

Frank Woolley in his pre-First World War prime

was amazed at Fielder's batsmanship at No.11, which so frustrated Arnold that he started swearing at him. Local glassblowers later presented the Kent pair with inscribed tumblers.

Woolley made his county debut in 1906, scoring 64 in the second innings. The great Johnny Tyldesley (295 not out) complimented him and kindly predicted that he would play for England. That red-letter day came three years later, and three years after that he took five Australian wickets in each innings at The Oval.

Frank colourfully described his duels with Australia's 1920s fast men. He reckoned that Ted McDonald bowled to hit him. He pulled him for six, then a bouncer hit the peak of his cap. Jack Gregory, with a new ball, even broke a disc in Woolley's back. But Harold Larwood still got his vote as the best of the fast men.

Talking required effort, even as he warmed to his reminiscences. The best bowling duo he ever saw was S.F.Barnes and Frank Foster during the 1911-12 Ashes tour. He remembered Barnes's fury in the opening Test when skipper Johnny Douglas took the new ball himself and was hit around: "Then he threw the ball to 'Barney'. He didn't try!"

Woolley despised the elephantine Aussie skipper Warwick Armstrong: "He wasn't at all a nice fellow . . . he cheated me once." Frank cut a ball to him at slip: "It hit the ground first but he threw it up. I said: 'Now then, Warwick, you didn't catch that!' He started swearing. But the umpire gave me out!" Television might have saved him.

The immortal Victor? "What I liked about Trumper was that when he had got a hundred against us, I said to him: 'You were in a hurry to get out, weren't you?' He said: 'Frank, there are three batsmen sitting in that pavilion as good as me. They want a knock, you know.'"

We returned to the matter of remuneration. He must have done well out

of the talent money that Kent used to pay out to the professionals? He did
. . . until the club decided he was doing too well and adjusted the scheme.
Frank protested to Lord Harris, stating that an American had just made him
a lucrative offer to play baseball. His Lordship sweet-talked him out of it by
promising a final testimonial that would surely match W.G.Grace's bonanza.
When the time came, Frank got only £900.

And now the talented Martha was putting together *Early Memoirs of Frank
Woolley*, a small limited edition, in the hope of making these twilight years a
little more comfortable. He died in Nova Scotia two years later.

*A stroke that brought Woolley a high proportion of his
astounding aggregate of 58,969 first-class runs (second only
to Jack Hobbs) – to which may be added 2068 wickets
and a record 1018 catches*

R.E.S.Wyatt
1901-1995
A Tough Theorist

BOB WYATT was the most serious old cricketer I have known. He was an incurable theorist and his condemnation of the lbw law was regularly hurled at anybody who happened to be in range. Like Don Bradman with his detestation of the front-foot no-ball law, Wyatt was destined to die unhappy that his pet conviction continued to be shunned by cricket's lawmakers. "Play forward and you're not lbw, but if you play back you're out!" Perhaps the increase in lbws under the Decision Review System might have calmed him. He also considered limited-overs cricket to be a prostitution of the game. What he would have thought of Twenty20 cricket hardly bears thinking about.

There was humour in him. He enjoyed recall of fielding in the deep at the MCG the day Bradman was out first ball in the Bodyline series. The barrackers had been boring him from the start with the taunt "You wait till Don comes in!" Cleverly Wyatt waited until Australia were nearly all out before turning

Wyatt (right) goes to the crease with Charlie Barnett during England's 1936-37 tour of Australia

to his tormenters and asking with mock innocence in his taut voice: "When's your Don coming in then?"

It was vice-captain Wyatt who had set the first Bodyline field at Melbourne some time before the first Test match of that stormiest of tours, while captain Jardine was away on a fishing break. Suspicious Australians believed that Jardine had absented himself in case the aggressive strategy failed. Wyatt always denied this. His unshakeable affection for Jardine was touching.

Sitting with him at Lord's in the 1980s, I mused over Percy Chapman's century there in the 1930 Ashes Test. "Missed first ball!" snapped Bob. Of course, he had been as deadpan a cricketer as Chapman had been jovial and carefree. When Wyatt replaced the much-loved Chapman as captain for the final Test of that 1930 series – in which the stupendous Bradman made 974 runs in his seven knocks – the new skipper had received unsavoury letters and even death threats, which he never forgot.

The anonymous taunters did not know their Wyatt. Physically and mentally he was as tough as they

Bob Wyatt, a bulldog of a cricketer

come. Nobody has recorded so many broken bones in the cause. The worst was the smashed jaw in the Jamaica Test of 1934-35. He seemed to be speaking from the side of his mouth as he recalled the bloody incident all these years later: "As they took me away on a stretcher I couldn't speak, so I motioned for some paper and a pencil and scribbled down a revised batting order."

Only three months later he was leading England against South Africa at Trent Bridge and scoring 149.

In that 1935 series he continued to annoy people. This time it was Tommy Mitchell, the bespectacled little Derbyshire legspinner, who showed his exasperation by telling Wyatt that he could not captain a box of tin soldiers. Not surprisingly the second Test at Lord's was Mitchell's last.

You had to be careful not to needle Wyatt. We were having a quiet drink during the South African Test Centenary celebrations in Johannesburg in 1989. I had been compiling a list of players who had been dismissed first ball in their maiden Test innings. In this very city in 1927 Bob had made a duck on his debut, but I couldn't trace details. So I asked him to search his memory. "Oh, no!" he assured me. There had been no such indignity . . . except that further research showed that there had been. Maybe it was not so much his pride as his memory that had failed him.

He must have approved of me, for he inscribed his biography: "With best wishes to a student of the game whose views coincide with that of the subject". I inherited from the author, the charming Gerald Pawle, the interview tapes for that book. They make lovely listening: two old chaps musing over the game and its characters from long-ago summers, with the friendly sound of clinking glasses in the background.

As so often happens, further questions spring up now that it is too late. Having heard a rumour that Gubby Allen was really Plum Warner's son, I put it to Bob Wyatt. His reaction: "Oh, we all knew that in the Thirties!"

Now I am left to wonder what precisely he meant: that they knew about the rumour, or that it was an established fact? Come back, Bob, please. There is one further question to be answered.

Old age comes to those who are lucky enough,
despite all the cricket injuries and broken bones:
R.E.S.Wyatt in South Africa 1989

These articles first appeared in *The Wisden Cricketer* and
The Cricketer between June 2007 and June 2012, with the
exception of the following, which have all been written
for this publication: David Bairstow, Tony Greig, Bill Hunt,
Frank Keating, Norman O'Neill, Peter Roebuck, and Syd Smith jnr.
There has been minimal amendment to the originals.

Index to Frith's Encounters